Publicly Funded R&D and Economic Development in Northern Ireland

D1325050

ISBN: 1 897614 56 X

© Northern Ireland Economic Development Office
Pearl Assurance House, 1-3 Donegall Square East
BELFAST BT1 5HB
Tel (028) 90232125 Fax (028) 90331250
e-mail: info@niec.org.uk   website: www.niec.org.uk

NORTHERN IRELAND ECONOMIC COUNCIL MEMBERS

Chairman: Janet Trewsdale

Members: *Independents*

Professor B Ashcroft
Professor R P Kinsella
P D Montgomery MA

Nominated by the Northern Ireland Committee of the Irish Congress of Trade Unions

F Bunting
P Holloway
J McCusker
M Morrissey

Nominated by the Confederation of British Industry for Northern Ireland and the Northern Ireland Chamber of Commerce and Industry

A Jackson FCA
R Johnston BA MBA
G P McGrath
N P E Smyth MSc C Eng MIMM
Bill Tosh

Director: P K Gorecki

CONTENTS

LIST OF TABLES AND FIGURES

List of Tables and Figures

ABBREVIATIONS USED

AFDS	Agri-food Development Service
AWT	Advisory Council on Science and Technology Policy
BBSRC	Biotechnology and Biological Sciences Research Council
BDS	Business Development Service
BRI	BioResearch Ireland
CCRU	Central Community Research Unit
CIP	Continuous Improvement Programme
CRI	Conference of University Rectors in Ireland
CSO	Chief Scientist Office
CSR	Comprehensive Spending Review
CST	Council for Science and Technology
CSTI	Council for Science, Technology and Innovation
DANI	Department of Agriculture for Northern Ireland
DED	Department of Economic Development
DEE	Department of Enterprise and Employment
DENI	Department of Education for Northern Ireland
DETI	Department of Enterprise, Trade and Investment
DETR	Department of the Environment, Transport and the Regions
DFP	Department of Finance and Personnel
DHFETE	Department of Higher and Further Education, Training and Employment
DHSS	Department of Health and Social Services
DoE (NI)	Department of the Environment for Northern Ireland
DSiP	Digital Signal Processing
DTI	Department of Trade and Industry

EA	Ministerial Committee on Economic Affairs
EASO	Cabinet Official Committee on Science and Technology
EC	European Commission
EHS	Environmental and Heritage Service
EPU	Economic Policy Unit
ESRI	Economic and Social Research Institute
EU	European Union
FP5	Fifth Framework Programme
FTE	Full-time Equivalent
GDP	Gross Domestic Product
GPA	Government Purchasing Agency
GR	Generic Research
HEFC	Higher Education Funding Council
HEFCE	Higher Education Funding Council for England
HEI	Higher Education Institution
HESIN	Higher Education Support for Industry in the North
HPSS	Health and Personal Social Services
HSS	Health and Social Services
ICSTI	Irish Council for Science Technology and Innovation
ICT	Information and Communication Technology
IDA	Industrial Development Authority
IDB	Industrial Development Board
IDBR	Inter-Departmental Business Registrar
IDC	Inter-Departmental Committee
IFI	International Fund for Ireland

IPS	Innovation Policy and Standards Directorate
IRTU	Industrial Research and Technology Unit
IU	Innovation Unit
JIF	Joint Infrastructure Fund
KEU	Knowledge Economy Unit
LEDU	Local Enterprise Development Unit
MAFF	Ministry of Agriculture, Fisheries and Food
MNE	Multinational Enterprise
MSTI	Minister for Science, Technology and Innovation
MTP	Manufacturing Technology Partnership Ltd
NCIHE	National Committee of Inquiry into Higher Education
NDPB	Non-Departmental Public Body
NERC	Natural Environment Research Council
NHS	National Health Service
NIAO	Northern Ireland Audit Office
NIBEC	Northern Ireland Bioengineering Centre
NICAM	Northern Ireland Centre for Advanced Materials
NICERT	Northern Ireland Centre for Energy Research and Technology
NICHE	Northern Ireland Centre for Diet and Health
NICS	Northern Ireland Civil Service
NIDevR	Northern Ireland Development of Research
NIEC	Northern Ireland Economic Council
NIERC	Northern Ireland Economic Research Centre
NIGC	Northern Ireland Growth Challenge

NIHEC	Northern Ireland Higher Education Council
NIIP	Northern Ireland Innovation Programme
NIKEL	Northern Ireland Knowledge Engineering Laboratory
NIO	Northern Ireland Office
NISRA	Northern Ireland Statistical and Research Agency
NITC	Northern Ireland Technology Centre
NUTEK	National Board for Industrial and Technological Development
OECD	Organisation for Economic Co-operation and Development
ONS	Office for National Statistics
OST	Office of Science and Technology
PATs	Programmes in Advanced Technologies
PES	Public Expenditure Survey
PGR	Post-Graduate Related
PPD	Product and Process Development Programme
PX	Ministerial Committee on Public Expenditure
QR	Quality Related
QUB	The Queen's University of Belfast
QUBIS	Queen's University Business and Industrial Services
R&D	Research and Development
RAE	Research Assessment Exercise
RDA	Regional Development Agency
RDO	Research and Development Office
RINNO	Regional Innovation Observatory
RIS	Regional Innovation Strategy

RITS	Regional Innovation and Technology Strategy
RITTS	Regional Innovation and Technology Transfer Strategy
RoI	Republic of Ireland
RRGs	Recognised Research Groups
RTC	Regional Technology Centre
RTDI	Research, Technological Development and Innovation
RTI	Research, Technology and Innovation
RTP	Regional Technology Plan
RUC	Royal Ulster Constabulary
S&T	Science and Technology
SABRIs	Scottish Agricultural and Biological Research Centres
SASA	Scottish Agricultural Science Agency
SHEFC	Scottish Higher Education Funding Council
SIF	Software Industry Federation
SME	Small and Medium-sized Enterprise
SNIFFER	Scotland and Northern Ireland Forum for Environmental Research
SOAEFD	Scottish Office Agriculture, Environment and Fisheries Department
SODoH	Scottish Office Department of Health
SOEID	Scottish Office Education and Industry Department
SPRU	Science Policy Research Unit
SQW	Segal Quince Wicksteed Ltd
STI	Science, Technology and Innovation
STIAC	Science, Technology and Innovation Advisory Council

STP	Science and Technology Programme
T&EA	Training and Employment Agency
TBNI	Technology Board for Northern Ireland
TCS	Teaching Company Scheme
TDP	Technology Development Programme
TEP	Technical Enterprise Programme
TICs	Technology Innovation Centres
TNO	Netherlands Organisation for Applied Research
TSFC	Tertiary Sector Funding Council
TVI	Technology Ventures Initiative
UCF	University Challenge Fund
UK	United Kingdom
UKWIR	United Kingdom Water Industry Research
UNE	Universities for the North East
UoA	Unit of Assessment
UU	University of Ulster
WDA	Welsh Development Agency
YHUA	Yorkshire and Humberside University Association

FOREWORD

In September 1998 the then Minister for the Economy, Adam Ingram, asked the Council, in the context of economic development, to review publicly funded relative to private Research and Development (R&D), to make national and international comparisons, and to advise on whether better co-ordination is desirable. More specifically, the Council was asked to advise on whether there are any duplications or gaps in publicly funded R&D such that maximum economic benefit is not being achieved and additional investment would be beneficial, and whether an inter-departmental mechanism to co-ordinate R&D programmes or a Minister with overall responsibility is required. This report presents the Council's findings and recommendations on these issues.

In 1993 the Council published a comprehensive report on private and public R&D, entitled *R&D Activity in Northern Ireland*, and the issue of R&D has featured prominently in many Council publications since then. A major concern of the 1993 report was a survey of private sector R&D activity, and this work is now undertaken regularly by Government. This report then concentrates on updating the 1993 report in the area of publicly funded R&D, and on recommendations concerning the overall co-ordination of R&D activity in Northern Ireland. In many ways findings and recommendations, perhaps not surprisingly, echo those of the Council's earlier report, within the context of the increasingly knowledge-driven economic development policy needs of today.

Publicly funded R&D is vital to success in an increasingly knowledge-driven economy. To do their own R&D and to be innovative, companies need access to publicly funded R&D through networking, co-operative research, and skills, training and knowledge transfers from public institutions such as universities. Innovation in the economy - the exploitation of new knowledge in new products and process - cannot exist in isolation from public investment in R&D in the science base and elsewhere.

The Council finds that in Northern Ireland there is quite an impressive array of R&D capabilities in both the public and private R&D spend, and some important co-ordination and collaboration initiatives. Much success has been achieved in the time since the Council's last report in 1993 in increasing industry R&D, in relating public R&D to the needs of industry and in improving links between Government, university and industry R&D and innovation. Initiatives such the Science Park, and others, promise more.

However, R&D strategy in Northern Ireland in the 1990s has concentrated on building up private sector R&D capabilities to the relative neglect of public sector capabilities. This is set to continue. The recently published proposed draft economic development strategy for Northern Ireland, *Strategy 2010*, contains a target of business expenditure on R&D of 1.5 per cent of GDP by 2010 but has no target for public spending on R&D. But it is highly improbable that business R&D can grow so substantially without the support of complementary growth in public R&D.

The Council's report finds, as did the 1993 report, that notwithstanding some excellent public and private capabilities in the economy, R&D in Northern Ireland, both public and private, is still too low, both in absolute terms and relative to major economic competitors, and there remains a lack of co-ordinated and complementary attention by Government in Northern Ireland to both public and private R&D in Government, industry, and the universities. Moreover, public R&D capabilities are not being exploited to their maximum economic potential. Much more needs to be done to fully integrate and co-ordinate all public and private R&D programmes so as to create synergy for economic benefit.

What is required in Northern Ireland is an R&D strategy that is a co-ordinated public-private partnership, directed by a dedicated unit of Government, with balanced and strategic attention to industry, Government and university R&D, channelled through a regional innovation strategy, and mainstreamed into a knowledge-driven economic development strategy. There is a great need for co-ordination of policy related to the public funding of R&D in Government Departments, universities and industry and in channelling that R&D to innovation. The report contains a detailed analysis of how publicly funded R&D can be taken forward within this agenda and it is on the basis of this analysis that the Council makes its recommendations to Government.

The Council would like to express its appreciation for the valuable assistance of Northern Ireland Civil Service Departments and Agencies in providing the input necessary for the completion of this report. The Council also benefited from the comments and advice provided by representatives of the Northern Ireland universities and Government officials and others outside Northern Ireland. The Council is grateful to the Industrial Research Technology Unit for meeting some of the external costs of producing the report.

Janet M Trewsdale
Chairman

1   INTRODUCTION

1.1   The dynamic factors that will unavoidably be driving economic development in Northern Ireland into the new millennium will be based increasingly on processes of knowledge creation and innovation. Local Research and Development (R&D) will be a critical input into these processes. Paradoxically, as the environment of R&D, innovation and economic development is becoming more global, knowledge capabilities at the local level are becoming more important to economic success. As noted by the recent United Kingdom (UK) White Paper on Competitiveness *Our Competitive Future: Building the Knowledge Driven Economy*, it is still the fact that "Intellectual breakthroughs ... cross hallways and streets more easily than oceans and continents" (DTI, 1998, Analytical Report, para 5.16). In other words, regions such as Northern Ireland can flourish by thinking globally and acting locally - by making critical local investments in knowledge production and utilisation capabilities, with local R&D as a key component. The local R&D and innovation system, when linked to national and international systems, can become the critical driver of local economic success, through the innovativeness of regional firms.

1.2   Government must invest in regional R&D. Not only can the public R&D spend improve public service delivery, but, in shaping the regional R&D strategy and in contributing to strong knowledge capabilities adequately channelled to innovation, it can make the economy more competitive and improve its attractiveness to indigenous and inward investment. R&D is a critical input, which Government can influence, into knowledge, and knowledge is critical to innovation and economic development. Public investment can lever significant private initiatives. However, public and private investment in R&D is not simply a matter of large sums of money *in*, improved public services and regional economic success *out*. The seeds sown must fall on fertile ground. The economic and social benefits of public and private R&D are increased the more cross-fertilisation of ideas, interdepartmental and interdisciplinary exchanges, networking, collaboration, co-operation, collective effort and co-ordination there is between researchers in Government, commerce and industry, the universities, and other academic and research institutions (Martin and Salter et al, 1996). The vitality and usefulness of the knowledge pool in Northern Ireland depends upon all institutions, public and private, replenishing it, sharing it and distilling from it.

1.3   The modern innovation process, within which R&D is a key component, has been described as a cat's cradle of complex interrelationships and networks of feedback connections (The Economist, 1999, pp.10-11). Various strands of public and private R&D inquiry might be strong but they might lead nowhere or be unconnected into regional, national and international R&D and innovation networks. Government's role is increasingly in fusing lines of inquiry, acting as a broker bringing greater co-operation, long-term consultative networking, collaboration and collective effort, and opening up the region to new opportunities and information. For R&D to make a significant impact upon knowledge exploitation and innovative economic development in Northern Ireland, public and private contributions must be effectively co-ordinated by Government, business and the universities and channelled to innovation.   The Northern Ireland Government's current strategy document for R&D states that "..within Government, industry and universities there is a shared and common interest in the effective delivery of a co-ordinated and focused strategy for R&D in Northern Ireland" (DED, 1992, p.7).

1.4   The Industrial Research and Technology Unit (IRTU), an agency of the Department of Economic Development (DED), directs Northern Ireland's public strategy for increasing private sector R&D activity, ensures its consistency with UK and European policy, and delivers it in collaboration with industry and higher education. An operating principle of IRTU is to work in partnership with other bodies, and a major objective is to increase private R&D in Northern Ireland and improve its linkages and networking, both internally and externally. In 1996, civil (non-defence) R&D in Northern Ireland amounted to approximately £152m, or 1.05 per cent of Gross Domestic Product (GDP), with approximately 52 per cent publicly and 48 per cent privately funded, and carried out in business (53 per cent), Government (13 per cent) and the universities (34 per cent)[1]. The overall level of R&D in Northern Ireland is low by national and international standards[2]. Notwithstanding the notable successes and accomplishments of IRTU in championing R&D and leveraging significant private investment during the 1990s, and some excellent public and private R&D capabilities in the economy, Northern Ireland remains very much a less-favoured region of both the UK and Europe in terms of R&D, knowledge creation, innovation and economic development. The potential of Northern Ireland is not being fully realised.

Focus of the Report

1.5   In asking the Council to undertake this project, the Minister for the Economy sought the Council's views on how the progress made in publicly funded R&D and its leverage of increased private R&D activity in Northern Ireland in the 1990s can be further built upon[3]. Are new structures and strategies of public funding delivery required, so that Government, universities and business in Northern Ireland can more effectively co-operate and collaborate towards the meeting of more challenging R&D, innovation and economic development targets? This report thus attempts to answer the following questions:

1.   Why is R&D, and in particular publicly funded R&D, important to innovation and economic development? (Section 3)

---

1   *For full details see Section 4 below.*

2   *Section 5 below.*

3   *It should, however, be noted here that public funding of R&D has been declining in Northern Ireland in recent years, in real terms, whereas it is private R&D that has been increasing. See Section 4 below.*

2.   What is a comprehensive estimate of publicly funded R&D activity in Northern Ireland in the 1990s, in relation to privately funded? (Section 4)

3.   How does public and private R&D activity in Northern Ireland compare with estimates of activity in the rest of the UK and elsewhere? (Section 5)

4.   What is the nature of co-ordination and co-operation in successful R&D systems elsewhere, between Government, universities and industry, in determining public R&D funding and in channelling publicly funded R&D towards innovation, competitiveness, and economic development? (Section 6)

5.   What is the nature of the private and publicly funded R&D system in Northern Ireland, and of co-ordination and co-operation between Government, universities and industry? (Section 7)

6.   Does there exist any unexploited potential for co-ordination and synergy in public funding of R&D in Northern Ireland, or gaps where additional investment would be beneficial, and is there an adequate level of co-ordination of R&D spending and programme delivery between Government, industry and the universities? (Section 8)

7.   Is Northern Ireland achieving maximum economic benefit from its public R&D spend? (Section 8)

8.   How might Government in Northern Ireland revise and develop its publicly funded R&D programmes to be better directed at innovation and competitiveness and at extracting maximum economic benefit in Northern Ireland? (Section 9)

9.   How might better co-ordination of R&D spending and

programme delivery between Government Departments, agencies, universities and business in Northern Ireland be secured? (Section 9)

10.   Is there a need for new institutions or mechanisms for strategic R&D funding and policy co-ordination in Northern Ireland, or for a new minister, office or agency with overall remit for regional R&D strategy and policy? (Section 9)

1.6   Of course, not all publicly funded R&D is solely, or even perhaps primarily, concerned with encouraging innovation, competitiveness and economic development. Much public R&D is concerned with statutory responsibilities for public service, in such areas as human and animal health, safety and welfare, and the environment. The public R&D spend in Northern Ireland must be viewed in light of these special public goals and responsibilities. However, this report concentrates on economic benefit. Even in the areas of health, agriculture or the environment, the R&D spend can contribute to economic prosperity through its channelling to innovation and commercial exploitation.

1.7   The Council is unable to evaluate and recommend the detailed how, what, where, when, who and why of publicly funded R&D in Northern Ireland. This is largely a matter for research staff in the Departments and elsewhere. The Report therefore concentrates on evaluation and recommendations concerning the overall publicly funded R&D system and strategy in Northern Ireland; on issues of coherence, consistency and co-operation, and on the channelling of publicly funded R&D to innovation and economic development through R&D strategy linked to and embedded within innovation and economic development strategy. In other words, is Government in Northern Ireland creating, encouraging and managing new knowledge in the right amounts and ways and channelling it to innovation so that maximum economic benefit can be secured, and, if not, how can policy performance in this area be enhanced?

Structure of the Report

1.8   Section 2 provides the definition of R&D used and illustrates the relationship between R&D and innovation. Section 3 follows with a review of the existing literature on the role of public and private R&D in regional innovation and economic development. Section 4 provides empirical estimates of public and private R&D in Northern Ireland, and Section 5 makes national and international comparisons. Section 6 presents for comparative purposes descriptions of the mechanisms for delivery and co-ordination of public R&D in other regions and national jurisdictions and establishes some bench-marks of best practice that can serve to evaluate present practice in Northern Ireland and to inform recommendations for the way forward.

1.9   Section 7 describes existing publicly funded R&D activities and initiatives in Northern Ireland and the Government-university-industry mix of activities. Section 8 makes an overall appraisal and assessment of the system of publicly funded R&D, especially insofar as it involves its co-ordination with private R&D and its channelling to innovation and economic development. Here the facts on Northern Ireland's publicly funded R&D system and strategy are assessed and the strengths and weaknesses of the system and strategy and its public-private funding mix are determined. An assessment is also made in Section 8 of whether there is a need for any revision in the structure, delivery and strategy of grant-aided and other publicly funded R&D in Northern Ireland, or for better co-ordination and co-operation between Government department, university and industry R&D funding and activity. Section 9 is prescriptive, and provides the Council's recommendations for future R&D policy in Northern Ireland.

2 R&D AND INNOVATION: DEFINITIONS AND ILLUSTRATIONS

Introduction

2.1   The focus of this report is on Northern Ireland's approach to publicly funded R&D as far as it relates to improving Northern Ireland's economic performance. Thus, the effectiveness of the R&D spend is examined in relation to its contribution to the commercial exploitation of new knowledge, or, in other words, innovation in the Northern Ireland economy. This section makes clear the distinction between the concepts of R&D and innovation and illustrates this distinction with some practical examples.

R&D

2.2   R&D is public and private investment in the generation of new knowledge. It is thus a tangible and measurable input of economic resources (See Box 1). This definition of R&D specifically excludes all activities involving the dissemination and application of existing knowledge such as routine scientific and technical testing and analysis, education and training, information services, and diffusion and utilisation of best practice, much of which is, of course, undertaken in the public sector in Northern Ireland. None of this is systematically oriented to the generation of new knowledge. As defined: "The guiding line to distinguish R&D from non-R&D is the presence ... of an appreciable element of novelty ... If the activity departs from routine and breaks new ground it should be included; if it follows an established pattern it should be excluded" (DED, 1997, Notes to Editors, Note 3).

Innovation

2.3   With R&D defined as investment in new knowledge creation, innovation can be defined as all of the scientific, technical, commercial and financial steps necessary for the successful utilisation of new

---

BOX 1

Definition of R&D

R&D includes **research** - all systematic work to increase the stock of knowledge, including knowledge of the behaviour of the material and physical universe, and of man, culture and society - and **development** - all systematic work to devise novel ways of using this increased stock of knowledge. It encompasses the mathematical and physical sciences, engineering and technology, medical and allied sciences, agricultural, biological, environmental and veterinary sciences, psychology, geography, economic and social studies, and the humanities. It involves gathering new information through theoretical conjecture, observation, experiment, measurement and deduction (research), and using this knowledge to devise new practical applications (development) - new or improved materials, products or devices, processes, systems, services, or solutions to problems. R&D can be further subdivided into:

Basic Research

- **pure**: research work carried out with no explicit orientation to economic and social benefits and with no effort to apply results to practical problems or to transfer results to sectors responsible for their practical application.
- **orientated**: research work carried out with the expectation that it will produce a broad base of knowledge relevant to the solution of practical problems or possibilities but with no attempt to devise any particular practical applications.

Applied Research

- **strategic**: research work that, although directed towards particular practical problems or possibilities, has not yet advanced to the stage where specific practical applications can be clearly identified and specified.

BOX 1 *continued*

Definition of R&D

- **specific**: research work which has specific practical applications - new or improved materials, products or devices, processes, systems, services or solutions to problems - as its explicit aims and intended outcomes.

Development

- systematic development work drawing on new knowledge and directed to how to implement the practical production or installation of new materials, products, processes, systems or services, or to how to improve those already produced or installed.

Source: DTI/OST (1998) Chapter 1, based on the Frascati definition

knowledge - the design, development and marketing of new or improved materials, products or devices, processes, systems, services or problem solutions. Innovation is thus the successful production, assimilation and exploitation of novelty in the economic and social spheres either in increasing the range of products and services available, or in introducing positive changes in management, work organisation, working conditions, and skills of the workforce (EC, 1995, p.9). It includes better education and training, telecommunications, infrastructure and environment. R&D is thus the generation of new knowledge that might feed into outputs: innovation is the productive act itself - the introduction of new knowledge and ideas into society, wherever they come from, in the form of new products, processes, services, and new value to customers and clients. Innovation encompasses technology transfer - the means by which new knowledge passes between organisations with a view to creating and developing new and commercially viable products and services.

The R&D and Innovation Relationship

2.4   R&D creates the new knowledge that can feed into technology transfer and innovation. It is technology transfer and innovation, largely but not exclusively in the private sector, that directly improves competitiveness, growth and development. In theory, local R&D is neither necessary nor sufficient for local technology transfer and innovation to take place. It might not lead to technology transfer and innovation[4] and one can, in theory, have innovation with no local input of R&D[5]. However, in practice, local inputs of public and private R&D are critical and necessary for regional technology transfer, innovation, competitiveness, and economic development. In turn, innovation is a critical factor, perhaps the most critical factor, in economic development, competitiveness, employment and prosperity[6].

2.5   Measurement of the local R&D input can serve as a proxy for innovation in the regional economy, but it is a poor proxy. The essence of innovation is the successful utilisation and commercial exploitation of new knowledge, not its creation. Local R&D is necessary but not sufficient for local innovation and is only one of several critical inputs. Many other factors other than local R&D, such as general framework policies that create a sound competitive environment for economic

---

[4]   *R&D is an input measure. Whether it leads to specific innovative outputs depends on technology transfer and commercial exploitation.*

[5]   *Through the input of R&D and the transfer of technology from outside the jurisdiction. 95 per cent of all world-wide R&D takes place outside the UK, 99 per cent outside Ireland, North and South.*

[6]   *Section 3 below provides a full analysis of these propositions. Of course, it is often difficult to make hard and fast distinctions between R&D, technology transfer and innovation, especially at the experimental development end of the R&D spectrum. The OECD estimates that R&D accounts for about one third of combined expenditure on R&D, technology transfer and innovation in the UK and other OECD countries (OECD, 1998a, Table 2.1, p.59).*

enterprise, managerial and marketing skills, social infrastructure, availability of skilled human resources and capital, and capabilities to adopt and adapt new technology from outside, influence local innovation. Moreover, it is a complex, risky and uncertain process by which inputs of local R&D can be transformed into innovations that can pass the rigorous tests of the marketplace and become expressed in quantifiable outputs such as patent registrations, favourable regional production and trade statistics, productivity growth and economic prosperity.

Illustrations of R&D and Innovation

2.6   The following examples, drawn from recent economic history, serve to illustrate the practical relationship between R&D on the one hand and innovation and economic development on the other.

*   There was a large R&D input into the invention of electricity and its practical application in the last quarter of the nineteenth century. AC and DC currents were perfected, transmission advanced by the invention of step-up and step-down transformers, and electric motors promised widespread application. These technologies, however, had to be commercialised via innovation into new products, processes, managerial organisations and institutions. The technological challenges had been largely overcome by the 1890s; challenges involved in commercialising these technologies on the factory floor and in the home played out in the period to the 1920s. It was only in the 1920s that the productivity improvements wrought by electrification brought the economic pay-off to this R&D and innovation.

*   A similar story could be told involving the invention and perfection of the internal combustion engine in the 1870s to 1890s through R&D and the mass production of the motor car through innovation and commercialisation by Henry Ford in the 1920s.

- Several decades of R&D went into the development of the microchip at Bell Laboratories and the Department of Defence in the United States in the 1940s to 1960s, and the development of the computer at IBM, AT&T and the Department of Defence. The full commercialisation of these products through innovation began only in the late 1970s. For example, adding the microchip, a new technology, to the typewriter, an existing product, led to the innovation of the word processor and its mass production and utilisation.

- Xerox Corporation, through much R&D, invented a mouse-windows-icon system for the personal computer in the 1970s but failed to exploit it commercially through innovation. It was Apple, Microsoft and Intel that produced the commercially viable products, processes, organisation and institutions to exploit this knowledge, the full economic productivity implications of which are still to be felt.

- The Internet was invented through R&D and first used non-commercially by the US military and universities. Companies such as Netscape and Microsoft have exploited some of the powerful marketplace potential of this technology through innovation. The returns to such innovation are forecast to be substantial.

- Large R&D efforts are currently being expended in, for example, the development of fuel cells that can turn fuel into electricity without combustion and might replace the internal combustion engine. Although the new knowledge is now being generated, the innovation that can turn this knowledge into commercially viable products is still some way off. The same is true in many current R&D programmes such as those in advanced materials and biotechnology.

2.7   Innovation around new sources of knowledge (such as in the examples given above) is perhaps the fundamental key to economic growth[7]. In order to innovate around new knowledge, however, the economy must contain within it local public and private capabilities, not only to be able to generate and understand new knowledge and its implications, but also to adapt it to local conditions and markets in order to turn it into socially and commercially successful new products, processes, organisations and institutions.

Conclusion

2.8   The relationship between R&D and innovation is often put in a simple way. R&D is using existing money (or economic resources) to create new knowledge; innovation is using this new knowledge to create new money (or economic resources). A positive economic return to R&D can then be thought of as ending up with more than you began with. This study is one primarily of publicly funded R&D in Northern Ireland (the original public input into the production of new knowledge) and not one of technology transfer, commercialisation and innovation (the successful implementation of new knowledge and ideas in all areas of business). Nevertheless, the report is much concerned with how publicly funded R&D in Northern Ireland is channelled into technology transfer and innovation, to create economic growth and prosperity.

---

7   *See Romer (1986, 1994). Harvard Economist Jeffrey Sachs, has recently stated "Modern society and prosperity rest on a foundation of modern science ... . Knowledge is becoming the undisputed centrepiece of global prosperity ..." (The Economist, 14 August 1999, pp.17 and 22).*

3   PUBLICLY FUNDED R&D AND ECONOMIC DEVELOPMENT

Introduction

3.1   The purpose of this section is to provide some general theoretical and empirical background to the contemporary role of publicly funded R&D in economic development.   After discussing some empirical estimates of the role of R&D in economic growth and employment, it goes on to outline the theoretical underpinnings of arguments for the need for local R&D capacity and, in particular, for public funding and co-ordination of local R&D activity.

R&D and Economic Growth

3.2   The Organisation for Economic Co-operation and Development (OECD) has recently stated: "Innovative efforts, and R&D in particular, are undoubtedly the major factor behind technical change and long-term economic performance" (OECD, 1998a, p.98). R&D is closely associated with product and process innovation and economic growth (Pianta, 1995). Regional investment in R&D has been shown to be one of the key factors behind disparities in the prosperity of European Union (EU) regions - a disparity that is six times greater for R&D than for any other indicator of prosperity between regions. Less developed regions are characterised by low R&D and a dominance of public over private R&D, poor connections to international research and innovation networks, and low levels of technology transfer both within the private sector and between the public and private sectors (EC, 1998). A factor common to regional economic success in Europe is the key priority given to innovation, into which local R&D is a key input (Dunford and Hudson, 1996).

3.3   In modern economic growth, product, process and service innovations are becoming increasingly knowledge and science-based, demanding more effective and relevant public and private R&D as an input (Lipsey, 1993). With the globalisation of markets for unskilled labour, regions such as Northern Ireland must move to higher value-added and skilled lines of production, and these lines require continuous innovation with R&D as a key component. Competitive advantage is being increasingly determined by acquired knowledge and skills rather than by nature-given endowments and hence can be increasingly shaped by R&D initiatives; regions can engineer long-run competitive advantage by investing in such inputs as R&D and human capital. Northern Ireland firms will lose out if they fail to develop new and better products, processes and services than their competitors. They are, therefore, increasingly dependent on public and private R&D as an input into this process, with more extensive inter-firm and public-private collaborations being demanded (Dunning et al., 1998).

3.4   The economic benefits of undertaking public and private R&D can be substantial. Measurement of private and social rates of return to R&D are not uncommon in the 20-50 per cent range[8]. For example, one recent study of R&D in the UK agricultural sector concluded: "regardless of methodology, or level of aggregation, the internal rate of return to UK R&D expenditures is estimated at around 20 per cent" (Khatri and Thirtle, 1996, pp.352-3). Another stated that: "... public agricultural investments have been shown to yield impressive social rates of return in numerous studies" (Hamilton and Sunding, 1998, p.830). The Economic Council of Canada (1992) estimated that 16 per cent of the growth of labour productivity in Canada, 1962-1990, was due specifically to national R&D expenditures. Freeman (1994) argues that 80 per cent of productivity growth is due to innovation, and 80 per cent of real output growth is due to productivity growth.

3.5   Hence, for economies to deliver rising productivity and living standards, greater emphasis must be placed on R&D, knowledge management and innovation. As stated in the recent UK White Paper on Competitiveness, "Those countries which adapt more readily and exploit the opportunities offered by the knowledge-driven economy will enjoy

---

[8]   *Griliches (1995).*

rising incomes and prosperity while those which lag behind may face relative economic decline" (DTI, 1998, Analytical Report, para 2.2). The future for economic growth in regions such as Northern Ireland thus lies in brains, not brawn or beauty.   CONCL'N

3.6   However, to be a fundamental input into regional economic development, public and private R&D must lead to technology transfer and to public and private innovation. Many commentators have noted the European Paradox that might also afflict Northern Ireland - the coexistence of substantial science and public and private R&D capacity and capability - the ability to create new knowledge - with the inability to transfer and transform this new knowledge into innovation and competitive advantage[9].

R&D and Employment

3.7   R&D expenditure and subsequent innovation have important employment impacts. Between 1994 and 1996, innovating companies in the UK showed considerably higher employment growth than non-innovating companies (ONS, 1998b)[10]. Firms that are innovators in Northern Ireland have experienced employment growth rates substantially higher than non-innovators[11], while research undertaken by the OECD

---

[9] *It has been argued that this is especially true in the European high technology sunrise sectors such as IT and electronics, in contrast to the same sectors in Japan and the United States. For example, the fax machine and the videocassette recorder were both invented in Europe in the 1950s but developed in Japan in the 1970s. The United States produces both knowledge and innovation; Japan is more concentrated on innovating around knowledge generated elsewhere. The specific situation in Northern Ireland is evaluated later in this report.*

[10] *25 per cent of innovating companies in 1996 also undertook R&D. No non-innovating companies did so.*

[11] *For details see Roper and Hewitt-Dundas (1998, Table 7.1, p.55). Innovators with respect to product innovations experienced employment growth of 19 per cent over 1993-95; non-innovators, 7.9 per cent.*

(1998a, Figure 1.13, p.51) shows that investment in Information Technology (IT) is positively related to employment growth. In the Republic of Ireland (RoI), externally-owned manufacturing firms that were R&D-active experienced a 16 per cent rise in employment, 1986-95, whereas firms that did no R&D experienced a 25 per cent fall. The corresponding figures for Irish-owned firms were a 31 per cent fall in employment for non-R&D performers, but only a 5 per cent fall for R&D active firms (ICSTI, 1998b, p.6).

3.8   Annual growth in employment by industrial sector in OECD countries between 1973 and 1990 was positively associated with annual growth in R&D expenditures, and EU Community Innovation Survey data show that annual growth in employment by industrial sector in the UK between 1970 and 1992 was positively associated with annual growth in both product and process innovation. Recent research on firms in the Mannheim Innovation Survey in Germany in 1995 shows that small and medium-sized enterprises (SMEs) that undertook R&D were more optimistic with respect to sales and employment and more export-oriented than SMEs that did no R&D. For example, 31 per cent of non-innovating companies exported, while 89 per cent of all companies with R&D departments did so. Recent research on United States small, medium and large-sized firms by the US Department of Commerce found that employment growth between 1982 and 1987 in all size categories was positively associated with sophistication of technology use[12].

3.9   Of course, it is not just a matter of employment growth, but also growth in well paid and sustainable employment. However, a more R&D intensive, innovative and knowledge-driven economy tends to result in better, more sustainable jobs and higher wages. Hence, R&D and its

---

12   *All findings in this paragraph are from a presentation by J M J Severijns at the Seminar "Innovation Policy and Strategy for Regional Progress in Europe", European Institute of Public Administration, European Centre for the Regions, Barcelona, 11-13 November 1998.*

utilisation in innovation clearly has an important role in realising sustainable employment at high wages in a modern economy such as that of Northern Ireland. Competitiveness is the only durable guarantor of job security in the long run. Long run competitive advantage and sustainable employment can be engineered from R&D and innovation and, for regions and firms committed to R&D and innovation, success tends to breed success.

Rationales for Public Funding and Co-ordination

3.10   Governments, including those of small regions such as Northern Ireland, must encourage local R&D. Michael Porter, among others, has convincingly argued that innovation is central to regional competitiveness, and Government can influence it through policies such as those relating to publicly funded R&D (Porter, 1990). Governments which support their regions' R&D system with substantial and well-targeted resources can make their regions more competitive in international markets.

3.11   Knowledge is fundamentally a public good[13], but it has other special characteristics as well. It is associated with increasing rather than diminishing returns and, after the initial investment to create it, it can be reproduced at little or no cost[14]. Generating new knowledge and being able to use it tends to be inter-linked. Moreover, with business and scientific communities more tightly knit on regional levels than on national and international ones, evidence tends to support the hypothesis that new knowledge and technology tend to diffuse into innovation most

---

[13]   *A public good is one that is non-rivalrous, non-excludable, and non-exhaustible; that is, the opposite to a private good, eg consider a piece of knowledge (public good) relative to a piece of chocolate (private good).*

[14]   *See Romer (1986). Thomas Jefferson's comparison of knowledge to a candle is pertinent here; as it lights another candle it does not diminish its own flame but instead the two candles shine more brightly.*

rapidly in its region of origin. The rise of the knowledge-based economy has made such attributes of knowledge a more salient concern than in the past. Although it is private companies that drive economic growth and prosperity, local Governments, in concert with business, universities, and other institutions can play a knowledge management role in regional economic development, aiding the local production of knowledge and its utilisation.

3.12   A way to view the positive economic return to undertaking local R&D is to consider the negative return that can be expected by not undertaking it. Special attributes associated with new knowledge creation and utilisation include learning-by-doing, the pre-emptive importance of being first and subsequent high barriers to entry, and increasing returns, such that new breakthroughs tend to feed on themselves to create further breakthroughs. Hence, a region that fails to invest in knowledge creation capabilities is likely to create a permanent and growing economic disadvantage for itself. Moreover, many modern production and service activities have no natural geographic base. They tend to gravitate to those regions that organise the knowledge creation and utilisation infrastructure to capture them and shun regions that do not. It is important to understand, however, just what it is in the regional R&D or knowledge creation process that demands a co-ordinated public input.

Overcoming Market Failure   Why Public?

3.13   The first and most traditional economic rationale for public funding of R&D lies in the notions of market failure and spillover. Incentives for private R&D are blunted, and hence the market fails, if firms are unable to appropriate a reasonable private return to their efforts. This can be caused by spillover. For example, successful researchers might leave to benefit other firms rather than the firm which undertakes the original research. More generally, firms will under-invest in R&D since social returns to R&D invariably exceed private returns - positive results benefit not just firms undertaking the R&D but also other firms and society in general, justifying a larger expenditure on R&D than that undertaken by private firms themselves and for their benefit alone. Moreover, firms tied to concerns of short-run profits and shareholder returns are more likely to under-invest in R&D. It is difficult for firms steeped in the technologies of today to see the significance of the technologies of tomorrow and firms collecting profits on existing technologies using existing assets and skills have a disincentive to try to move to new ones. But they must be encouraged by Government to do so, since no advantage lasts forever. If Northern Ireland companies, in co-operation with their Government and universities, do not work to make their existing products and processes obsolete, their competitors in other regions will.

3.14   There is thus a role for Government and university R&D to fill in gaps of private under provision, especially in basic and strategic research. It is imperative that regional Governments, in their funding of R&D, take a long and economy-wide view of the knowledge creation process, and not, as firms might, a view based on the short-term interests of the firm alone. In the Northern Ireland context, the public authorities must also take into account the dearth of large-scale enterprise and corporate headquarters in the economy and the dominance of SMEs. Small firms are often loath to invest in R&D due to high fixed costs and uncertain returns[15]. Any R&D strategy in Northern Ireland should thus address the need for SMEs to increase their access to publicly funded R&D in Government and universities. There are also, of course, other market failure and public good considerations that demand a public input into R&D, such as public health and safety and environmental concerns.

---

[15] *SMEs (less than 200 employees) accounted for 66 per cent of private sector employment (excluding agriculture) in Northern Ireland in February 1999 and enterprises of less than 50 employees accounted for 97.4 per cent of all private sector enterprises (excluding agriculture) (DED, 1999).*

Encouraging Knowledge Network Participation

3.15   Another rationale for public R&D funding is its role in providing linkages between sources of new knowledge to encourage new interactions and networks between regional, national and international expertise and information (Martin and Salter et al, 1996). In other words, Government can use its influence to broaden and deepen the regional knowledge pool and its linkage to external pools. The social and economic benefits of a knowledge network are increased the larger the network and the more agents use the network. For example, the more people use the Internet the more benefit there is to each user[16]. However, each business will link to such a knowledge network only on an assessment of its own private costs and benefits, ignoring the social benefits of their connection. There will, therefore, be under-networking in the absence of public policy[17]. As a result, Government can encourage participation and collaboration in the regional pool of new knowledge that is so crucial to economic development by acting as a facilitator and animator of participation in regional, national and international knowledge networks (Braczyk, Cooke and Heidenreich, 1998; Cooke, 1996, 1998; Cooke and Morgan, 1998).

---

16   *Moreover, if every home and business was linked to the Internet or some other system of knowledge and information of the future, this might affect the physical layouts and materials flow patterns of goods and services production and have as profound an influence on productivity as the power, transportation and universal education systems investments of the past, reaping at least as high and systemic social rates of return (See David (1990) and Katz and Shapiro (1994)).*

17   *National science and technology (S&T), R&D and innovation, continuous education and training, and information superhighway networks, all infrastructures that rank at least equally as important as the more physical infrastructures of roads, airports and schools, are often cited to fall into the category of gateway infrastructures with significant network externalities, where public investment and funding can lever significant private participation and economic and social benefit.*

Establishing Regional R&D Capability

3.16   Government must work to build up regional R&D capability. The local R&D infrastructure is substantially more important to regional innovation and economic development than foreign infrastructures. Linkages with external R&D are no substitute for internal regional capability because, in order to fully understand and utilise knowledge generated elsewhere, regions must have some knowledge capability of their own. The basic level at which innovation flourishes is the local level, and although what constitutes 'local' requires definition on a case-by-case basis, the capacity to innovate locally is dependent on the agglomeration of specialised skills, knowledge, institutions and resources that make up the appropriately defined local technological infrastructure or knowledge pool (Feldman, 1994). In this infrastructure, both private and public R&D are critical components; for the knowledge pool to develop, public-private partnership is essential. Furthermore, public and private R&D complement rather than substitute for each other. With growing industrial expenditure on R&D, companies increasingly need access to publicly funded R&D and to the personal and tacit knowledge, professional networks and post-graduate training that publicly funded R&D provides[18]. As noted by the OECD; "As industrial research has come to focus increasingly on the solution to specific short-term problems, large firms that previously conducted basic research in their own laboratories are tending to outsource long-term research to universities" (OECD, 1998b, p.71).

3.17   Inward and indigenous investors see the regional R&D system

---

[18]   *As noted recently by Harvard Economist, Jeffrey Sachs, "Advances in science and technology not only lie at the core of long-term growth, but flourish on an intricate mix of social institutions - public and private, national and international ... Free-market ideologues notwithstanding, there is scarcely one technology of significance that was not nurtured through public as well as private care", The Economist, 14 August 1999, pp.16,17.*

and strategy as critical components of the regional support infrastructure for industry. In particular, the encouragement of local high technology companies depends critically on the local R&D infrastructure, and especially the research base in universities, which companies must have available to dip into as the need arises. Moreover, another important conduit and infrastructure for local knowledge creation is foreign direct investment[19]. Ideally, inward investment should be characterised by knowledge-driven companies that are willing to develop R&D links with local companies, which are based on mutual sharing of knowledge and involving collaborative interaction to accelerate new product and process development. Most regional authorities attempt to 'embed' mobile capital and ensure that its contribution to local economic upgrading moves beyond simple job creation to the formation and development of mutually reinforcing R&D and innovation linkages with the local economy. There is clear recognition that inward investment "brings world class production techniques, technical innovation and managerial skills which can be transferred to local companies" (DED, 1995, p.19). A commonly used indicator of embeddedness of inward investment is the extent to which a plant has a local R&D capacity[20]. Especially beneficial are firms that finance free-standing laboratories and research institutes in the local economy, and interact with local universities and other institutions.

3.18   Within the regional publicly funded R&D infrastructure, there is strong evidence that the local provision of high quality higher education

---

[19] *In 1998 there were approximately 390 foreign-owned businesses in Northern Ireland employing 57,700, or 9.5 per cent of all employees in the economy - 123 were RoI-owned and 111 USA-owned (DED, 1999).*

[20] *A recent Council survey of inward investment plants in Northern Ireland found that 57 per cent of respondents had this capacity (NIEC, 1999a). This compares with a figure of 41 per cent from the Council's 1991 R&D Survey (NIEC, 1993). To the extent that this represents a trend, it would be encouraging. A recent NIERC report examines the developmental potential of such linkages in more detail, focusing on knowledge transfers from Multinational Enterprise (MNE) plants to their local suppliers (Crone and Roper, 1999).*

teaching and research is critical in strengthening the local economy. Detailed localised knowledge is an important benefit of a local university capability. Knowledge links between industry, Government and universities are facilitated by proximity. Local knowledge infrastructure, especially university research capabilities, is strongly and positively correlated with the flow of new inward investment and the embedding of that investment fully into the regional economies[21]. The increasing role of knowledge in economic development is working to increase the contribution that universities can make to economic growth in their regions, since the activities in which they engage - research, teaching, and technology transfer, or the production, transmission and transfer of knowledge - are at the heart of the knowledge-based economy (Thanki, 1999).

3.19   Universities represent 30 per cent or more of the national R&D efforts of some OECD countries (OECD, 1998b). Technology transfer to companies, which see universities as source of knowledge to be exploited for commercial purposes, is the dominant pattern of collaboration between industry and universities, and is increasingly regarded as an important and legitimate function of universities, "in addition to their more traditional roles of producing knowledge [research] and transmitting it [teaching and training]" (OECD, 1998b, p.71). Moreover, "entrepreneurship ... is one of the principal mechanisms for knowledge transfer from universities to the business sector" (p.74) through spin-out company formation. Of course, universities must work to ensure that their production, transmission, and transfer of knowledge are kept in balance and mutual reinforcement (p.76). Moreover, public-private R&D

---

[21] *However, the need to provide a full range of disciplines locally for students, government and industry makes it more difficult for universities to specialise in areas of strength and exploit niche opportunities. It is a difficult task for university research funding to promote relevant and broadly-based research capability, collaborations and links with business, government and other research users, and the generation of revenue from research grants and contracts.*

collaboration through universities is best balanced with public and private research capabilities, for example in research institutes, outside universities.

3.20   Best (1999, in process) illuminates the vital role of public and private R&D capability in regional economic development. In Best's view, regional economic development is driven by entrepreneurial firms. These firms, and this process of development, is critically dependent on the pool of knowledge available regionally, which in turn is critically dependent not only on the firms' internal capabilities but also on investment in R&D and skill-formation by the regional authorities. Entrepreneurial firms develop out of the regional knowledge base and the R&D partnering capabilities it offers. Especially important are regional public and private capabilities in engineering and science, capabilities that play critical roles in upgrading the technological and skill base of the region. In particular, regional research universities are perhaps the critical intermediary institutions of the new economy, just as financial institutions were of the old.

Overcoming Systemic Failure through Co-ordination

3.21   A final fundamental economic rationale for public funding of R&D is its role in resolving systemic failures in the local knowledge pool through co-ordination. The R&D environment is increasingly global and interdisciplinary, and the process of innovation for firms and public institutions is increasingly complex, involving more stages and more agents. Firms working on large-scale projects with long-term outcomes are increasingly reliant on external sources of knowledge, joint-ventures, international strategic alliances, and cost-sharing. Hence, in funding regional R&D and encouraging regional innovation, regional Governments must work to facilitate beneficial co-operation and co-ordination between firms, universities and Government and encourage beneficial linkages with external sources of knowledge. In other words, they must work to establish and strengthen the connections within the regional R&D infrastructure (Pilat, 1998). In a knowledge-driven economy, there is need for fusion of Government, industry and university R&D at the regional level (Best, 1995). The quality of regional industry R&D is enhanced by associations with other public and private R&D in universities, Government, and other industries through networking and co-operative research.

3.22   Much of this co-ordination rationale for public intervention in R&D is based on the burgeoning literature on the regional 'learning economy' (Hudson, 1999; Storper, 1997; Maskell and Malmberg, 1999; Morgan, 1997; and Maskell et al, 1998), and the notion of interactive learning (Lundvall, 1992). This argues that high cost regions can sustain competitiveness and prosperity in the global economy through "knowledge creation and the development of localised capabilities that promote learning processes" around "learning by interacting" (Maskell and Malmberg, 1999, p.20). There is growing acceptance of the notion of a 'learning society' in which "A major priority of government-backed research must be to enrich the global knowledge base by backing science and technology in universities and research institutions ... [and] ... facilitating the diffusion and application of knowledge ..." (Vickery, 1999, p.10). Recent research on innovation in high technology SMEs in Europe finds that such firms greatly benefit from collective learning in their regions in the form of knowledge transfers between firms and knowledge centres such as universities (Keeble and Wilkinson, 1999).

Conclusion

3.23   The regional authority's role in publicly funding local R&D is thus to resolve regional systemic failures, eliminate mismatches, facilitate and strengthen linkages, networks and co-operation, and fill in the gaps and missing links in the regional R&D system. A public R&D regional strategy must be devised to sharpen the focus and efficiency of public spending (Lopez-Bassols, 1998). Governments must seek to direct regional R&D strategy towards matching priorities and specialisations closely with the regional pattern of international competitive advantage in commerce and industry (Porter, 1990). Regional authorities must maximise the local economic impact of their R&D funding through specialisation and co-ordination with private funding through mechanisms such as technology foresight. The potential to shape R&D, and hence innovation and economic development, at the local level gives regional Governments an influence in the knowledge-led economy of the present, for good or bad, that was unimaginable in many of the economic processes of the past (Best, 1999, in process). Government must synchronise its own R&D activities with those of business and the universities in order to create the learning economy needed for high productivity and economic growth.

3.24   However, regional Government's R&D strategy must be grounded in the actual R&D capabilities of the region's entrepreneurial firms, and the capabilities they can develop, within the regional system, since it is the region's entrepreneurial firms that ultimately drive regional economic development forward. Close Government-industry-university links in R&D and innovation are required (Pilat, 1998)[22]. Important Government priorities lie in improving access for SMEs to regional knowledge networks and in diffusing best business practice to them (Vickery, 1999).

3.25   The efficiency of public and private R&D spending, and how they combine with improved strategies for channelling R&D into innovation and integrating new knowledge in industrial and commercial operations, is becoming more important than the size of public and private

---

[22]   *As stated recently in the financial press "The idea is that companies are more successful if they co-operate as well as compete. It is hoped that by bringing businesses into contact with each other and with public agencies and universities, and by sharing knowledge, skills and technologies, innovative energy [and hence economic development] can be unlocked" Financial Times, "New Ways to Help Industry", 23 October 1998, Brian Groom).*

R&D budgets per se. For example, the competitive turnaround of United States high technology industries in the 1990s was, arguably, due more to improved strategies for integrating R&D results into industrial innovation, rather than to any increase in R&D spending (Pilat, 1998). However, the commitment of public funding to local R&D remains important. The foundation and genesis of regional competitive advantage lies in both the public and the private domain. Thus, it is imperative that regional R&D is conducted in a co-ordinated and co-operative manner between the public and private sectors. Regional Government must take the initiative to improve policy design and delivery in their management of an efficient and co-ordinated regional R&D system within an appropriately holistic R&D, innovation and economic development strategy.

3.26   In the OECD, trends include a falling level of real financing and expenditure on R&D by Government, and a fairly flat level of private sector expenditure (OECD, 1998a). The Government share of financing of business R&D has dropped to around 10 per cent of the total (Vickery, 1999). Michael Porter's recent research results suggest that R&D expenditure by business is more productive in terms of economic growth and productivity than Government and university expenditure, but that Government funding of R&D in universities and business is beneficial (Porter, 1998). Moreover, Porter finds that a high Government share of total economy-wide R&D personnel has a negative influence on productivity. Public initiatives to raise private sector activity, especially in SMEs, via grants and other assistance, are useful methods to redress any imbalance in this respect. However, private sector R&D activity must be supported by public sector activity - to do their own R&D and to be innovative, companies need access to publicly funded R&D through networking, co-operative research, and skills, training and knowledge transfers from universities and other public institutions.

4   R&D IN NORTHERN IRELAND: EMPIRICAL ESTIMATES

Introduction

4.1   Before examining in detail publicly funded R&D activity in Northern Ireland it is necessary to obtain a comprehensive estimate of total expenditure on R&D in the economy, and to find out how that total has changed over the last number of years, in answer to the question posed in the introduction to the report (No 2, page 4).

4.2   Since 1993, there have been two primary sources of estimates of R&D funding and expenditure in Northern Ireland:

(i)   annual Office for National Statistics (ONS) estimates for all regions of the UK, including Northern Ireland, based on a sample of 64 Northern Ireland firms, and on estimates for Government departments and universities; and,

(ii)   triennial DED estimates, carried out by the Statistics Research Branch of DED on behalf of IRTU, for 1993 and 1996[23], and based on a survey of approximately 380 firms and estimates for Government departments.

Thus, the most recent estimates for which both surveys can be compared is for 1996. Since they give somewhat different answers due to differences in coverage and estimation techniques, the purpose of this section is to describe and reconcile these sources. For the reader who wants to avoid the detailed statistical discussion, the outcome is presented in the conclusion to this section.

---

[23] *The next survey will be carried out in 2000 for expenditures in 1999.*

ONS

4.3   The ONS estimates of expenditure on intramural R&D 1993-1996 in cash terms (current pounds) are presented in Table 4.1. These are the estimates given in the ONS publications *Regional Trends* and *Economic Trends*. These are estimates of R&D activity performed *within* the business, Government and higher education sectors. Although much of the information is based on ONS business and Government R&D surveys, information on expenditure for local authorities (eg health authorities) and those areas of Central Government not available from the Government survey is also utilised.

TABLE 4.1

ONS Estimates of Expenditure on Intramural R&D in Northern Ireland, by Sector of Performance, 1993 to 1996, Current £

	1993 £m	1994 £m	1995 £m	1996 £m	% Increase 1993-1996
Business	39	58	61	83	+113
Government Establishments	15	18	18	23	+53
Higher Education	38	50	52	57	+50
Total	92	126	131	163	+77

Source: Central Statistical Office/Office for National Statistics <u>Regional Trends</u>, various issues

4.4   Full results from the Government survey and compiled by the ONS are published by the Department of Trade and Industry (DTI) in its annual *Science, Engineering and Technology Statistics*. These estimates differ from those in *Regional Trends* in that they also include Government extramural spending (eg R&D grants to business) but exclude information obtained outside the Government survey, such as local and health authorities' spending.

4.5   Figure 4A depicts the distribution of the £23.4m in Government

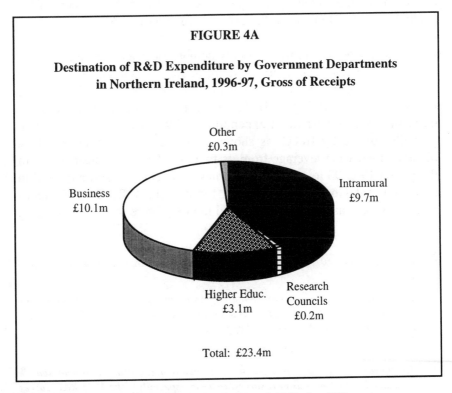

FIGURE 4A

Destination of R&D Expenditure by Government Departments in Northern Ireland, 1996-97, Gross of Receipts

Other
£0.3m

Business
£10.1m

Intramural
£9.7m

Higher Educ.
£3.1m

Research
Councils
£0.2m

Total: £23.4m

Source: DTI/ONS (1998, Annex 2, Table 2, p.103)

intramural and extramural expenditure on R&D in Northern Ireland in 1996 (gross of receipts), as estimated by the ONS Government survey[24]. This shows that £10.1m of business expenditure was publicly funded, Government department contracts worth £3.1m were carried out in higher education institutions (HEIs), and £9.7m was intramural (within Department) spending[25]. It is this £9.7m in intramural spending plus an estimated £13m in health authorities R&D spending that makes up the £23m shown in Table 4.1 as total intramural Government establishments spending in 1996, as published in *Regional Trends* and *Economic Trends*. Prior to 1996, Government intramural spending in Table 4.1 was made up of intramural department spending plus an estimate of 1.5 per cent of the health budget (DTI/ONS, 1998, Table 6.1, footnote 4, p.61).

4.6   The ONS Government survey demonstrates a downward trend in real intramural and extramural funding of R&D (including IRTU R&D grants) by Government in Northern Ireland, 1993-94 to 1997-98, net of receipts, as shown in Figure 4B[26]. This can be contrasted to the upward trend in business intramural expenditure, 1993 to 1996, promoted and partially funded by IRTU, as shown in Table 4.1[27]. IRTU has thus obtained increasing leverage from its funding of R&D in businesses. In the period 1992-93 to 1998-99, there has also been a downward trend in real recurrent Government funding for university R&D in Northern Ireland, in contrast to an upward trend in GB (Figure 4C). For example,

---

[24] *Receipts totalled £0.6m and hence the net of receipts figure estimated for 1996 was £22.8m.*

[25] *The Government department expenditure of £3.1m in higher education in Figure 4A is contract research only and, of course, excludes Department of Education for Northern Ireland (DENI) block funding for university research.*

[26] *Again this excludes non-contract based university block funding.*

[27] *The upward trend shown in Table 4.1 is probably overstated due to poor sample coverage by the ONS business survey, in 1993 especially. The 1996 R&D survey carried out by DED (see Table 4.2 below) estimates a more modest rise in business expenditure, 1993-1996, of 43 per cent in nominal and 31 per cent in real terms.*

Government funding for university R&D in Northern Ireland was reduced by £4m in 1997-98[28].

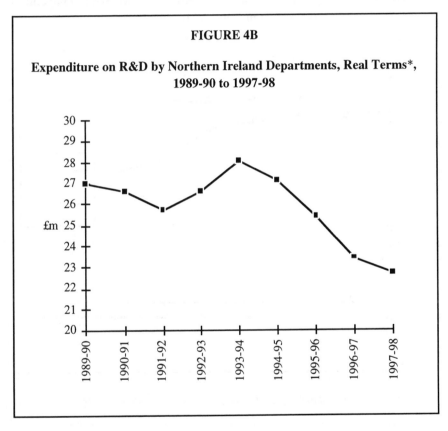

FIGURE 4B

Expenditure on R&D by Northern Ireland Departments, Real Terms*, 1989-90 to 1997-98

* Adjusted for inflation.

Source: OST (1999, p.66)

---

28 *For further commentary on these changes see NIEC (1997). On university R&D see McKenna and Hogg (1998).*

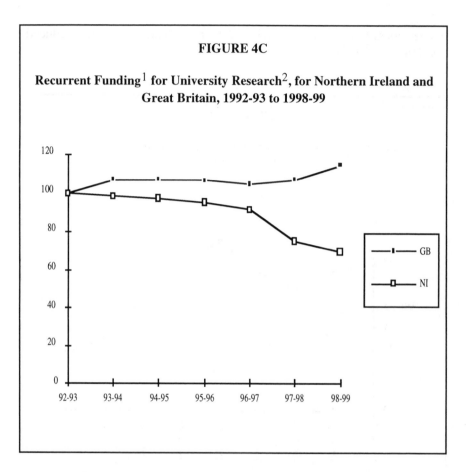

FIGURE 4C

Recurrent Funding[1] for University Research[2], for Northern Ireland and Great Britain, 1992-93 to 1998-99

[1] *Expressed in Constant £, using GDP deflator, 1992-93 = 100.*

[2] *For 1997-98, some Higher Education Funding Councils have consolidated part of their previous capital grants and teaching funds for research students into the research funding formula. The figures in the above graph exclude this funding to enable comparisons with previous years to be made.*

Source: Based on data provided by DENI to Professor McKenna, University of Ulster.

DED

4.7   The DED R&D funding and expenditure estimates for 1993 and 1996 are based on a comprehensive census of business activity and information from Government, but they do not provide estimates for funding and expenditure in universities. The latter must be added to the DED figures to get an overall estimate of R&D funding and expenditure in Northern Ireland[29]. The DED estimates are shown below in Table 4.2,

TABLE 4.2

DED Estimates of R&D Expenditure, Northern Ireland, 1993 and 1996*

		1993 (£m)	1996 (£m)
1.	Industry - Total Civil	60	86
	a. Self-Funded	49	71
	b. Government-Funded	11	15
2.	Government (Other)	14	14
3.	Total Civil	74	100
4.	Defence	n/a	9
5.	Universities	n/a	n/a
6.	Total	74	109

* *There are no data available for Defence in 1993 and the Total for R&D expenditure in 1993 assumes that Defence is zero.*

Source: DED (1997)

---

[29]   *The incorporation of estimates for universities in the 1999 R&D survey is currently under consideration.*

again in cash terms. They are substantially below the corresponding ONS estimates in Table 4.1, since they omit university expenditure. Of note, however, is the much higher estimate of total business expenditure in 1993 of £60m than the 1993 ONS estimate of intramural business expenditure of £39m. This can be explained by the inclusion of business extramural expenditure in the DED estimates, and the improved coverage provided by the DED census of that year relative to the sample coverage of the ONS survey.

Reconciliation and Consolidation

4.8   The differing and alternative estimates of R&D in Northern Ireland can be a source of some confusion. An example of this appeared in the Dearing Report on funding for higher education where it is stated that university research accounts for 64 percent of total R&D in Northern Ireland, compared with 23 percent for the UK as a whole (NCIHE, 1997, Main Report, p.455)[30]. This figure has passed into common parlance and is certainly wrong. It is derived by expressing the total research income of the Northern Ireland universities in 1993-94 of £47m, derived from the Department of Education for Northern Ireland (DENI) information, as a percentage of the DED estimate of total R&D in Northern Ireland in 1993 of £74m, from Table 4.2 above. This is 64 per cent. However, the cash figures in the numerator and denominator are not comparable - the DED total excludes DENI block grants to the universities and most other university funding, which the university research income figure includes. Hence the 64 per cent figure is, in effect, expressing apples as a share of oranges. The correct figure for the proportion of R&D in Northern Ireland undertaken in the universities is, as shown below, and demonstrated in the ONS estimates in Table 4.1, approximately 34 per

---

[30] *Following publication of the Dearing Report, DED informed IRTU that the figure quoted for university R&D as a proportion of all R&D in Northern Ireland was inaccurate.*

cent[31]. This is a high figure relative to EU and OECD national proportions as is discussed below in Section 5, but not exceptionally high[32].

4.9   Confusion and ambiguities, and the fact that there are alternative empirical estimates based on differing coverage and estimation techniques, indicate that there is a need for reconciliation and consolidation of the figures for R&D funding and expenditure in Northern Ireland. Table 4.3 attempts such a reconciliation and consolidation in order to derive an overall figure.

Government and Industry

4.10   With defence spending of £9m included, the DED estimate of total business and Government expenditure on R&D in 1996 of £109m (line 4, DED, plus line 10, Table 4.3) is £13m or 13.5 per cent higher than the ONS estimate of £96m (line 4, ONS, Table 4.3 which includes defence)[33]. Part of this discrepancy is explained by the fact that DED also includes extramural business spending. Also, DED calculates a total of £15m in Government support for business R&D in 1996, whereas ONS

---

[31] *As discussed in more detail below. The 64 per cent figure is misrepresentation enough, yet even that has been prone to exaggeration, eg the then Vice-Chancellor of QUB, Sir Gordon Beveridge, wrote "Northern Ireland is quite different from GB in that the two universities here together provide almost the entire research base", 26 March 1997, Belfast Telegraph. Current Vice-Chancellor of QUB, Professor George Bain, is quoted in the Belfast Telegraph as stating "Queen's itself provides 50 per cent of all R&D in Northern Ireland", 28 September 1998.*

[32] *See Tables 5.2 and Table 5.3 in Section 5. University R&D, as a share of total R&D, exceeds 30 per cent only in Austria, Spain, Portugal and Greece, but is close to 30 per cent in Belgium and The Netherlands.*

[33] *The ONS estimate here is made up of £83m business intramural expenditure (Table 4.1), £10m of which was funded by Government (Figure 4A), and the remaining £13m of Government funding (Figure 4A).*

TABLE 4.3

Reconciliation of ONS and DED Estimates of R&D Expenditure in Northern Ireland, 1996

		ONS £m	DED £m
1	Industry - Total	83	86
	a. Self-Funded	73	71
	b. Government-Funded	10	15
2	Government (Other)	13	14
3	Government Total	23	29
4	Total (Net)	96	100
		96	
5	Health Authorities	12	
6	Total Industry and Government (Net)	108	
7	Universities: Total	52	
	a. Block Grant	27	
	b. Government Contracts	4	
	c. Health Authority Contracts	2	
	d. Industry Contracts	2	
	e. Other External Sources including Research Councils	17	
8	Total University (Net)	44	
9	**Total Civil (Net)**	**152**	
10	**Defence**	**9**	
11	**Total**	**161**	

Total University (Net) = 7 - (7b + 7c + 7d) or 7a + 7e.
Total Civil (Net) = 6 + 8.
Total = Total Civil (Net) + Defence

Source: NIEC Estimates

and IRTU figures (Figure 4A and Section 7 below) show only an expenditure of £10-£11m. In 1996 DED counted approximately £4m of Industrial Development Board (IDB) expenditure as support for R&D whereas it might be more properly classified as selective capital assistance for industrial investment. In 1993, 96 per cent of all Government support for business R&D was estimated to come from IRTU (DED, 1997, Annex 5). However, these 1996 DED figures argue that only approximately 63 per cent of R&D support was from IRTU, with 30 per cent from IDB, whose remit does not include funding for R&D. Removing this £4m in IDB capital assistance from the R&D figures reconciles the ONS and DED estimates somewhat[34]. Any remaining difference between the figures is thought by DED to be due to the superior coverage of their census estimation method relative to the ONS sample survey methodology.

4.11   £12m in R&D expenditure in 1996 in the health authorities (line 5, Table 4.3) should be added to the figure of £96m (which represents DED estimated business and Government non-defence expenditure with the £4m noted above removed). This £12m expenditure is counted in the ONS intramural Government estimates published in *Regional Trends* (Table 4.1 above) but is not counted in either the ONS or DED Government survey estimates (Figure 4A and Table 4.2 above). Health sector R&D expenditure is counted in the ONS estimates for 1997-98 (see Figure 4D relative to Figure 4E)[35]. Total Health and Personal Social Services (HPSS) expenditure is examined in more detail below, but Figure 4E shows that it was estimated to be about £12.7m in 1997-98 (the Department of Health and Social Services (DHSS) total of £14m minus

---

34 *However, at the time of the 1996 R&D survey, the £4m funding by IDB was queried by DED Statistics Branch and validated by contacting the companies concerned.*

35 *These figures are net of receipts estimated at £0.6m in 1996-97 and £1.0m in 1997-98.*

FIGURE 4D

R&D Expenditure Net of Receipts by Departments in Northern Ireland, 1996-97

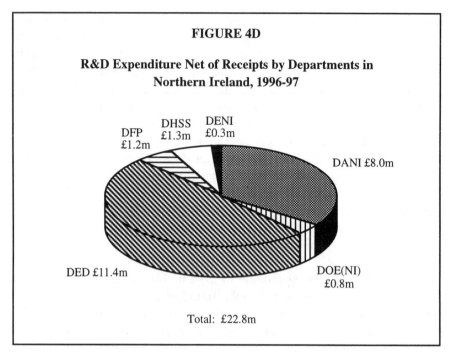

Total: £22.8m

Source: DTI/ONS (1998, Annex 2, Table 1, p.103)

£1.3m DHSS intramural expenditure[36]). An estimate of £12m for 1996 (implicit in the ONS intramural Government estimate in Table 4.1) brings total Government department expenditure up to £35m (line 3, ONS, plus line 5, Table 4.3) and total net Government department and industry expenditure up to £108m in 1996 (line 6, Table 4.3)[37].

---

[36] *The predominant share of HPSS R&D funding before 1998 was allocated under the Supplement for Teaching and Research. It is now allocated through the Research and Development Office of the HPSS. See Section 7 below.*

[37] *It should be noted here that funding for HPSS R&D has been set at £8.4m for 1998-99 and £9.1m for 1999-2000, much below the estimate of £12m for 1996-97. See*

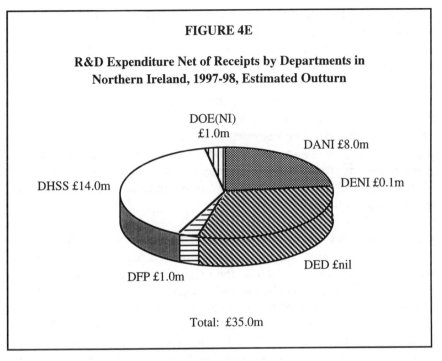

FIGURE 4E

R&D Expenditure Net of Receipts by Departments in Northern Ireland, 1997-98, Estimated Outturn

DOE(NI) £1.0m

DANI £8.0m

DHSS £14.0m

DENI £0.1m

DED £nil

DFP £1.0m

Total: £35.0m

Source: DTI/ONS (1998, Annex 2, Table 1, p.103)

Universities

4.12   An estimate of additional expenditures in universities (ie The Queen's University of Belfast (QUB) and the University of Ulster (UU)) must be added to the Government and business expenditure figures to obtain an overall estimate of R&D expenditure in Northern Ireland. Again the distinction between R&D funders and doers must be made

---

HPSS (1999). The £12m expenditure in 1996-97 was also corroborated in a written answer to a question in the House of Commons, Hansard, written answers, 3 February 1999, p.608.

clear. Some expenditure in the universities is funded by Northern Ireland Government, health authorities and industry through research contracts, and hence is already accounted for in Government and business intra and extramural expenditure (line 6, Table 4.3). For example, QUB reports research expenditure funded by Northern Ireland health authorities in 1996-97 of £1.7m, presumably in the Faculty of Medicine and Health Sciences, where the medical faculty has joint arrangements with the DHSS[38]. The DHSS reports research expenditure of £2.6m in 1997-98 and £2.3m in 1998-99 involving "grants and project costs in respect of non-routine investigations into various aspects of the operation of the HPSS, most of which are carried out by outside agencies such as university departments"[39].

4.13   In 1996 a new method was established to estimate public funding of R&D in universities, using grant income as a proxy for expenditure. Research-oriented grants include the Quality Related (QR) block grant and other grants deemed to be used for research, for example, one-third of Post-Graduate Related (PGR) grant plus fee funding. Table 4.4 attempts an estimate of the Research Quantum going to the Northern Ireland universities in 1996, based on DENI figures (Hughes, 1998). On the basis of the universities' Research Assessment Exercise (RAE) results and non-formula based research funding (one-third of PGR), QUB and UU were allocated a QR block grant of approximately £16m in 1996. Northern Ireland Development of Research (NIDevR) funding was about £9m, and capital grants allocated to research were around £2m, giving a total of approximately £27m[40].

---

[38]   *Hughes (1998, Table 9, p.15).*

[39]   *DFP/HM Treasury (1998, p.341).*

[40]   *NIDevR was cut by £4m to £5m in 1997-98 and there was no capital funding, so the block grant fell to £23m. The grant goes about two-thirds to QUB and one-third to UU.*

TABLE 4.4

University Research Funding, Northern Ireland, 1996

	£m
Block Grant	
Quality Related: Block	16.0
Quality Related: NIDevR	9.1
Joint Research Equipment Initiative	0.5
Capital Grant	1.9
Total Block Grant	**27.5**
Other Funding	
NI Government Contracts	4.2
GB Government Contracts	0.7
EU Funds	5.4
NI Health Authorities' Contracts	1.7
GB Health Authorities' Contracts	0.2
Research Councils	5.0
UK Charities Contracts	4.0
Industry Contracts	2.0
Other Overseas Sources	0.7
Other Sources	1.0
Total Block Grant and Other Funding	**52.4[1]**
Net of NI Government, Industry and Health Authority Contracts	**44.5[2]**

[1] *Corresponds to line 7, Table 4.3.*
[2] *Corresponds to line 8, Table 4.3.*

Sources: Hughes (1998, Tables 1 and 2, p.6, and Tables 9 and 10, p.15) and HEFCE (1998, Table 12, p.25)

4.14   Other research income in the universities came from a variety of sources, for example, contracts from the Northern Ireland Government amounted to £4.2m, from Northern Ireland health authorities, £1.7m, from industry, £2m, EU funds of £5.4m, UK charities funding of £4m and £5m from Research Councils. Total research income thus combined in 1996 to about £52m. Net of Northern Ireland Government department, industry and health authority funding, totalling £8m, the additional expenditure contribution of the universities to Northern Ireland R&D expenditure was thus approximately £44m. In Table 4.3 contract income from Northern Ireland Government (£4m, line 7b), health authorities (£2m, line 7c) and industry (£2m, line 7d) are subtracted from total university research incomes (£52m, line 7) to obtain a total of £44m net additional university expenditure (line 8). This is made up of the block grant for research from DENI of £27m (line 7a, the Research Quantum), and £17m in other external sources of research expenditure (line 7e), including EU and International Fund for Ireland (IFI) funds, UK research council and charities funding, GB health authorities and departmental funding, and other overseas sources (see Table 4.4).

Overall Total

4.15   With total R&D expenditure in Northern Ireland accounted for in this way, civil expenditure totalled £152m in 1996 or 1.05 per cent of a 1996 GDP at factor cost of £14,470m (ONS, 1998c, Table 12.1, p.145). Defence expenditure undertaken in business adds £9m, for a total of £161m, or 1.11 per cent of GDP. These figures can be compared with those recently reported in the draft economic development strategy, *Strategy 2010* (Economic Development Strategy Review Steering Group, 1999, p.117), for business, Government and higher education R&D in Northern Ireland, adding to 1.0 per cent of GDP.

4.16   Figures 4F and 4G show the estimated distribution of civil (non-defence) R&D funding and expenditure in Northern Ireland. Private

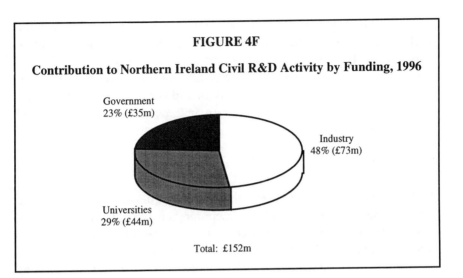

FIGURE 4F

Contribution to Northern Ireland Civil R&D Activity by Funding, 1996

Government
23% (£35m)

Industry
48% (£73m)

Universities
29% (£44m)

Total: £152m

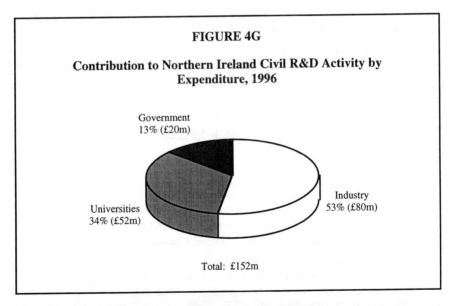

FIGURE 4G

Contribution to Northern Ireland Civil R&D Activity by Expenditure, 1996

Government
13% (£20m)

Industry
53% (£80m)

Universities
34% (£52m)

Total: £152m

Source for both Figure 4F and 4G: NIEC estimates

industry funded approximately 48 per cent of civil R&D in 1996, with the public sector (Government departments, and Non-Departmental Public Bodies (NDPBs) such as hospitals and universities) accounting for the other 52 per cent. On an expenditure or activity basis (Figure 4G), 53 per cent of civil R&D was carried out in industry, 34 per cent in the universities, and 13 per cent intramurally in Government departments and NDPBs, such as hospitals[41].

Conclusion

4.17   This section answers the second question posed in the introduction to the report: what is a comprehensive estimate of publicly funded R&D activity in Northern Ireland in the 1990s, in relation to privately funded? The DED R&D and innovation strategy document, *Innovation 2000*, published in 1992, reported Northern Ireland spending on R&D at 0.5 per cent of GDP[42]. The Council's 1993 report on R&D contained in it a comprehensive survey-based estimate of total R&D expenditure in Northern Ireland in 1991-92, and at that time, the Council found that total publicly and privately funded (Government, university and industry) R&D in Northern Ireland was £80m or 0.8 per cent of GDP (NIEC, 1993).

4.18   The estimates derived in this section show that civil R&D activity in the Northern Ireland economy totalled £152m or 1.05 per cent of GDP

---

41   *Teaching and research staff in the Department of Agriculture and Food Science at QUB are considered to be DANI employees and hence much of DANI R&D expenditure, which is, in fact, the majority of Government department activity, could be attributed instead to the universities through the QUB-DANI link (see Section 7 below). This would increase the university contribution somewhat above 34 per cent.*

42   *It is clear that this figure did not include university expenditure. This same figure is used to represent total R&D expenditure in 1996 in Northern Ireland in many recent Government documents, eg the <u>IDB Corporate Plan, 1998-2001</u> (IDB, 1998, p.20), <u>IRTU Corporate Plan, 1998-2001</u> (IRTU, 1998, p.12) and the <u>Forward Look 1999</u> (OST, 1999, p.31).*

in 1996. Over half of this activity (£80m or approximately 0.55 per cent of GDP) took place in the private sector, £7m or approximately 10 per cent funded from public sources through grants and other support for business R&D. Of the activity that took place in the public sector, the large majority was undertaken in the two universities (£52m or approximately 0.36 per cent of GDP). The remainder (£20m or approximately 0.14 per cent of GDP) took place in Government departments and NDPBs such as hospitals. With regard to Government appropriations (public funding) for civil R&D, this totalled approximately £79m or 0.54 per cent of GDP, with private sector funding another £73m or 0.51 per cent of GDP. Defence R&D spending adds £9m for a total R&D activity in 1996 of £161m, or 1.11 per cent of GDP.

5   R&D IN NORTHERN IRELAND AND OTHER JURISDICTIONS: EMPIRICAL ESTIMATES

Introduction

5.1   In order to put R&D expenditure in Northern Ireland in perspective, it is important to compare it, in total and in composition, with R&D expenditure in other regional and national jurisdictions. This section then attempts to answer the question posed in the introduction to the report: How does activity in Northern Ireland compare with estimates of R&D activity in the rest of the UK and elsewhere? Such comparisons can serve to provide useful bench-marks from comparable economies elsewhere, and suggest goals for policy in Northern Ireland, although care must be exercised in making sure that scope, coverage and definitions of R&D used are also comparable across economies.

UK Regions

5.2   In the UK context, useful comparison can be made between R&D expenditure in Northern Ireland and that in Scotland, Wales, the North East, Yorkshire and Humberside, and Merseyside. Table 5.1 presents some summary economic statistics for Northern Ireland and these other regions, all of which are similarly northern or western and therefore somewhat peripheral to the dominant centres of economic activity and R&D expenditure in the UK, ie the Midlands and South-East of England.

5.3   Figure 5A shows ONS figures on intramural business, Government and higher education R&D expenditure in 1996 for Northern Ireland and these other regions of the UK, and Figure 5B expresses these figures in per capita terms, and includes the UK averages. These figures show that the balance between business, universities and Government is approximately similar across the regions. In per capita terms, however (Figure 5B), Northern Ireland has the second highest regional level of Government expenditure on R&D per capita (behind Scotland), the lowest level of university expenditure, and the second lowest level of business expenditure (behind Wales). The more devolved nature of Government in

TABLE 5.1

Comparative Economics Statistics, Selected Regions, UK, 1996-1998

	GDP per Head, 1996 Relative to UK Average (%)	Claimant Count Unemployment Oct 1998 (%)	Population, 1996 (m)	Index of Manufacturing Productivity, 1996, UK=100
NI	81	7.3	1.7	84
Scotland	99	5.6	5.1	108
Wales	83	5.5	2.9	109
North East	85	7.3	2.6	103
Y'shire & H'side	89	5.6	5.0	93
Merseyside	73	8.9	1.4	109

Source: DTI (1999, Tables 1(a), 2 and 7(b)(i) p.35, 36, 45)

Northern Ireland might explain the higher per capita levels of Government expenditure, and the industrial structure of Northern Ireland is normally cited to explain the relatively low level of business expenditure. The low level of university expenditure on R&D per capita reflects a relative shortfall in university research funding due, in part, to the Northern Ireland universities' performance in the Research Assessment Exercise. Per capita figures for all of these regions, including Northern Ireland, are, however, well below the UK averages, with the exception of per capita expenditure on R&D in Scotland in universities.

5.4   Figure 5C shows ONS figures for 1996 on R&D employment in business and Government as a percentage of the regional labour force in

Northern Ireland and these other regions of the UK, as well as in England. Approximately 1,800 Full-time Equivalents (FTEs) were engaged in R&D in business in Northern Ireland in 1996, and 200 FTEs in Government. Both of these figures, when expressed as a percentage of the regional labour force, are relatively low in the UK context.

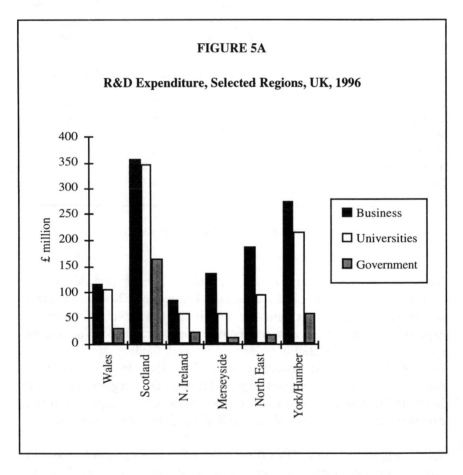

FIGURE 5A

R&D Expenditure, Selected Regions, UK, 1996

Source: ONS (1998a, Table 14, p.67)

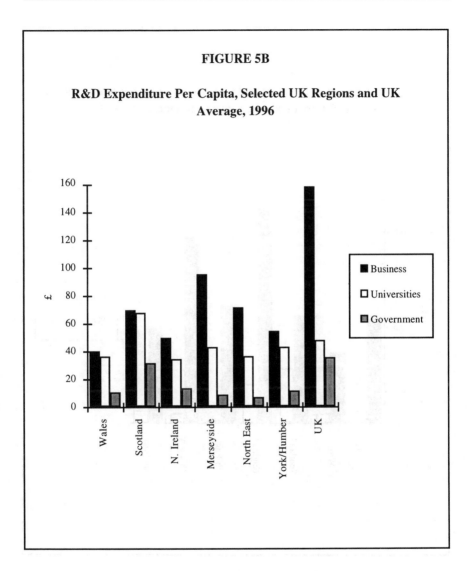

FIGURE 5B

R&D Expenditure Per Capita, Selected UK Regions and UK Average, 1996

Source: ONS (1998a, Table 14, p.67)

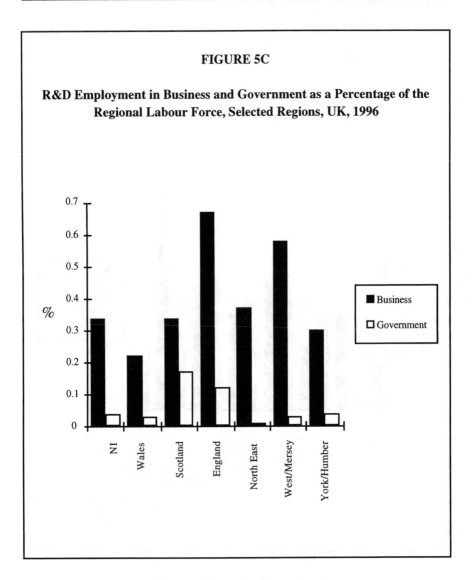

FIGURE 5C

R&D Employment in Business and Government as a Percentage of the Regional Labour Force, Selected Regions, UK, 1996

Source: ONS (1998a, Table 15, p.68)

European Nations

5.5   Table 5.2 places the estimates of Section 4 of Northern Ireland expenditure on civil and defence R&D as a percentage of GDP, and GDP per capita, in comparison with EU national figures. Expenditure on total R&D at 1.11 per cent of GDP in Northern Ireland is well below nations such as Denmark (1.82 per cent), Norway (1.65 per cent) and the Republic of Ireland (1.41 per cent), but similar to Italy (1.04 per cent), and above Spain, Portugal and Greece[43]. There appears to be a strong positive relationship between relative expenditure on R&D and relative GDP per capita.

5.6   Table 5.2 also shows the distribution of civil and defence R&D expenditure across business, Government and higher education, by sector of performance.   Business, Government and higher education performance of R&D in Northern Ireland, at 0.61, 0.14 and 0.36 per cent of GDP respectively, are all low in comparison with EU national averages. For example, higher education R&D as a per cent of GDP is lower in Northern Ireland than the UK national average (0.39 per cent), and lower than in all other EU nations except the Republic of Ireland, Italy, Spain, Portugal and Greece. Business performance of R&D in Northern Ireland looks especially low in an EU context, and is only 61 per cent of the level (as a share of GDP) of expenditure in the RoI.

---

[43]   *It is also below the UK average of 2.05 per cent, the EU national average of 1.84 per cent and the OECD average of 2.16 per cent, but similar to expenditure in New Zealand (1.03 per cent). Caution must, however, be expressed in comparing these figures across different sources, with scope and coverage broadly comparable but not identical.*

TABLE 5.2

Expenditure on R&D as a Per Cent of GDP, 1995, by Performing Sector and Relative GDP per Capita, Selected Countries and Northern Ireland, 1998

	Business (%)	Government (%)	Higher Education (%)	Total (%)	GDP per Capita (UK=100)[1]
Sweden	2.68	0.13	0.63	3.45	112
Finland	1.50	0.41	0.46	2.37	106
France	1.44	0.49	0.38	2.34	106
Germany	1.51	0.34	0.43	2.28	113
Netherlands	1.09	0.37	0.58	2.06	105
United Kingdom	1.34	0.30	0.39	2.05	100
Denmark	1.10	0.32	0.41	1.82	143
Belgium	1.09	0.06	0.44	1.61	106
Austria	0.83	0.12	0.50	1.58	114
Ireland	1.00	0.14	0.27	1.41	97
Northern Ireland[2]	**0.61**	**0.14**	**0.36**	**1.11**	**81**
Italy	0.56	0.22	0.26	1.04	88
Spain	0.37	0.17	0.25	0.80	61
Portugal	0.12	0.16	0.21	0.61	46
Greece	0.11	0.13	0.22	0.48	49

[1] *Relative GDP per capita figures are expressed at market exchange rates, and relative to the UK=100.*

[2] *Northern Ireland figures are for 1996 (see text).*

Sources: EC (1998, Table 1), NIEC estimate, OECD (1999, pp.12-13) and DTI (1999, Table 1(a), p.35)

G7 and Other Nations

5.7   Table 5.3 shows the percentage distribution of total civil and defence R&D activity by sector of performance in Northern Ireland and in the entire UK and the other G7 countries, in 1996. On a sector of performance basis, the Northern Ireland universities do account for a

TABLE 5.3

International Comparison of Gross Civil and Defence Expenditure on R&D by Sector of Performance, G7 and Northern Ireland, 1996

	Sector of Performance (Per Cent)				
	Government	Business	Higher Education	Other	Total
NI	**12.4**	**55.3**	**32.3**	~	**100**
UK	14.4	64.9	19.5	1.2	100
Germany[1]	15.3	65.8	18.9	~	100
France	20.4	61.5	16.8	1.3	100
Italy	19.9	57.7	22.4	~	100
Japan[2]	10.4	70.3	14.5	4.8	100
Canada[3]	14.9	62.2	21.7	1.2	100
USA	9.0	72.7	15.1	3.3	100

[1]   *Data for "other" included elsewhere.*
[2]   *Data are for 1995.*
[3]   *Excludes most capital expenditure.*

Sources: DTI/ONS (1998, p.72); NIEC estimate

higher proportion of civil and defence R&D activity in Northern Ireland (32.3 per cent) than do higher education institutions in the whole of the UK and other nations of the G7 (19.5 per cent in the UK, and ranging from a low of 14.5 per cent in Japan to 22.4 per cent in Italy). The figure for the proportion of expenditure undertaken in business in Northern Ireland (55.3 per cent) is correspondingly low in comparison with the UK and other G7 national averages (ranging from 57.7 per cent in Italy to 72.7 per cent in the USA).

5.8 Table 5.4 compares the percentage of civil and defence R&D

TABLE 5.4

International Comparison on Source of Funding of R&D, G7 and Northern Ireland, 1996

	Source of Funds (Per Cent)	
	Public (Government, Universities and Other)	Private (Business Enterprise)
NI	**54.6**	**45.4**
UK	52.7	47.3
Germany	39.4	60.6
France*	51.7	48.3
Italy	50.5	49.5
Japan	27.7	72.3
Canada	51.8	48.2
USA	38.6	61.4

* Data for France are for 1995.

Sources: DTI/ONS (1998, p.73); NIEC estimate

funded, rather than performed, by the private relative to the public sector for Northern Ireland, the UK, and the other G7 nations[44]. Public funding as a percentage of total expenditure is relatively high, over 50 per cent, in the UK, including Northern Ireland, and in Italy, France and Canada, and relatively low, under 40 per cent, in Germany, Japan and the United States.

5.9   Table 5.5 provides information on Government appropriations for civil (non-defence) R&D as a percentage of GDP for Northern Ireland, the UK, the RoI, and other national jurisdictions, in 1996. This shows that Northern Ireland is above the UK average for Government appropriations for civil R&D as a percentage of GDP and above appropriations in the RoI, Canada, USA and Japan. However, Northern Ireland is well below the level of priority given to civil R&D by the Governments of Australia, Denmark, Finland, Germany, Iceland, France, the Netherlands, Norway, and Sweden.

Conclusion

5.10   The picture of R&D in Northern Ireland that emerges in UK regional and other national comparisons, and in answer to the question posed in the introduction to the report, is that of a low overall expenditure, and a relative dominance within this low expenditure of public sector funding and performance. Table 5.2 shows that less developed nations of the EU are characterised by low R&D and a dominance of public over private R&D (Northern Ireland, Italy, Spain, Portugal, Greece). More successful nations undertake more R&D and especially more private sector R&D (eg Sweden). However, Table 5.5 shows that EU nations with high public appropriations for civil R&D do appear to generate significant private R&D, employment and economic

---

[44]   *Assuming that the £9m in defence expenditure undertaken by business in Northern Ireland in 1996 was publicly-funded. Again, scope and coverage of the figures are broadly comparable but probably not identical.*

TABLE 5.5

Government Appropriations for Non-Defence R&D as a Percentage of GDP, Selected Countries, 1996

Finland	0.95
Sweden	0.92
Germany	0.82
Iceland	0.79
France	0.77
Netherlands	0.76
Denmark	0.74
Norway	0.73
Australia	0.64
NI	**0.54**
Japan	0.53
UK	0.49
USA	0.42
Canada	0.38
RoI	0.36

Sources: OECD (1998c); NIEC estimate

growth (Finland, Sweden, Germany, France, The Netherlands, Denmark). On average in the EU, Government funds 39 per cent of national R&D efforts (ICSTI, 1999a, p.16). Such evidence supports a conclusion that it is the private sector that largely drives innovation, economic growth and prosperity, but public support for R&D in businesses, universities, Government departments and NDPBs is also critical in regional economic development. Commitment to R&D, and commitment of public funding for R&D, do appear to be important to economic performance[45]. The fact that public commitment to R&D in Northern Ireland is a relatively high proportion of overall public and private R&D spending, but that this overall spending is relatively low, highlights the importance of this study. Private sector R&D expenditure is low, and must be increased, but publicly funded R&D also plays a critical role in overall R&D, innovation and economic development.

---

[45] *For a similar conclusion based on a more detailed empirical analysis, see Porter (1998).*

6   COMPARATIVE PUBLICLY FUNDED R&D SYSTEMS AND STRATEGIES

Introduction

6.1   Before moving to an assessment of the publicly funded R&D system and strategy in Northern Ireland and recommendations for the way forward, this section presents some brief case studies of approaches elsewhere in the UK and Europe. Publicly funded R&D in Northern Ireland is first placed in its national, EU and island context, through a brief overview of the UK, EU and RoI approaches to publicly funded R&D policy, as they have evolved in the 1990s. The section then goes on to describe publicly funded R&D systems, strategies and policy practices in some UK and European regions and nations of particular interest to Northern Ireland, given economic similarities and proximities; Scotland, Wales, the North-East, Yorkshire and Humberside, South Sweden, Denmark and the Netherlands. Models of comparative practice are established with a view to informing description and assessment of the system and strategy in Northern Ireland (Sections 7 and 8) and to suggesting policy innovations that might be considered for Northern Ireland (Section 9). For the reader who wishes to avoid the details of the case studies, common themes and alternative models are presented in the conclusion to this section.

The UK, EU and RoI

United Kingdom

6.2   The UK economic development strategy, as set out in the 1998 Competitiveness White Paper *Our Competitive Future - Building the Knowledge-Driven Economy* (DTI, 1998), centres around knowledge as the key to economic growth. The Minister for Science, the Office of Science and Technology (OST), and the DTI Innovation Policy and Standards Directorate (IPS), working with the Innovation Unit (IU) and others, champion science and technology (S&T) and innovation and co-ordinate Foresight and Inter-Departmental R&D. The OST takes an active role in promoting partnership, collaboration and collective effort, as do Foresight Panels and the new Ministerial Science Group[46]. Knowledge management in the UK is further bolstered by a reconstituted Council for Science and Technology (CST).

6.3   The Minister for Science was appointed and the OST established in 1992. The 1993 White Paper *Realising Our Potential* (DTI, 1993) established the UK science, engineering and technology strategy for the 1990s[47]. The thrust of the White Paper was that R&D capabilities in the UK were strong, but were not being adequately channelled to innovation and increasing economic competitiveness. There was a perceived lack of co-ordination between Government departments on R&D funding, and Government overall was deemed not to be working adequately with industry and science to set national priorities. The outcome was the Forward Look process for departments (an annual review of Government-funded R&D), and Technology Foresight, now known simply as Foresight because of its much broader scope. Both managed by the OST, these initiatives were to inform policy and spending decisions across Government, to target Government programmes for collaborative R&D and knowledge transfer, to avoid duplication of effort, and to induce collaboration and co-operation.

6.4   Forward Look estimates for Government R&D spending did not appear over the last two years due to the change in Government and the Comprehensive Spending Review (CSR), but were published again in July 1999. The latest Forward Look (OST, 1999) outlines the roles, priorities and spending of the public bodies responsible for S&T in the UK over the next three years. In its role of taking an overview of S&T

---

[46] *The Blueprint for the next round of Foresight was published in December 1998 and sets out the Government's plans for taking forward the Foresight Programme to November 2000.*

[47] *This was the first review of S&T strategy since the early 1970s Rothschild Report and government response.*

activities in the economy and in its mission to maximise their contribution to economic and social welfare, the priorities of OST are:

- to maintain the excellence of the publicly funded science base in the UK via the Research Councils and in co-operation with the Higher Education Funding Authorities and others, through, for example, reviewing the dual support system with regard to ensuring that it delivers quality, relevance and cost-effectiveness, and developing indicators to measure the performance of the science base and its exploitation;

- to promote, in co-operation with DTI and others, business exploitation of the science base to generate sustainable economic and social development, through, for example, the Foresight Programme and commercialisation of research outputs from public sector research establishments;

- to promote the effective use of science across Government to maximise the benefit of public research expenditure, including developing information on the outcomes of expenditures; and,

- to encourage UK participation in international S&T activity that promises to be of economic and social return to the UK.

As argued by the Minister for Science, Lord Salisbury, in his introduction, *Forward Look 1999* "shows that our priorities are being addressed in a coherent way across Government and are not confined by narrow departmental boundaries" (OST, 1999, p.iv).

6.5   The CSR science conclusions were published in July 1998 (HM Treasury, 1998) and "will result in a real terms increase in total Government expenditure on science of nearly 11 per cent by 2001-02" (OST, 1999, p.iv), including an extra £700m for the Science Budget, coupled with £400m from the Wellcome Trust. Of the £700m, £300m was the public sector contribution to establish a £600m Joint Infrastructure Fund (JIF) jointly with the Wellcome Trust, designed to revitalise UK science and engineering research, buildings and equipment; £300m was to support new and enhanced Research Council programmes, mainly in universities; and £100m was for other infrastructure support, including a contribution to a new high intensity X-ray facility, to which the Wellcome Trust had pledged an additional £100m. Two further initiatives have also been announced aimed at enhancing exploitation of university research; University Challenge - over £60m of seed capital funding for taking forward exploitable ideas to a stage where they can be spun off or licensed commercially, half of which was provided from the Science Budget; and Science Enterprise Centres - £25m from the Science Budget to establish about eight centres of enterprise within the UK with the goal of turning good research into good business. The CSR also announced an additional £100m support for university research in England via the Higher Education Funding Council for England (HEFCE), half of which has been used to enhance the JIF explicitly for English universities. Budgets for Northern Ireland, Scotland and Wales were also enhanced[48]. As Prime Minister Tony Blair noted in the Foreword to HM Treasury (1998): "... because our future success depends on knowledge, creativity and innovation, we have found new money for science, universities and the arts ... to meet the challenges of the new economy".

6.6   The OST's dual roles are to administer the Science Budget by providing the Director General of the Research Councils and to provide policy advice to Government on S&T strategy and priorities; it plays no role in the financing or administration of R&D spending in Government

---

[48] *These increases hence also apply to Northern Ireland, but the CSR for Northern Ireland did not explicitly mention science and technology (DFP/HM Treasury, 1998), except to say (p.21) that the Northern Ireland universities "... have access, on the same basis as other UK institutions, to a new Wellcome Trust OST Research Fund to support research in science and technology".*

departments. Until 1999, the main official forums for the discussion of S&T issues of cross-departmental interest were the Cabinet Official Committee on Science and Technology (EASO) which had representation from all the main S&T spending departments, the Ministerial Committee on Economic Affairs (EA) (including S&T), the Chief Scientific Advisor's bilateral meetings with Departments on expenditure and input into the Ministerial Committee on Public Expenditure (PX). However, EASO is currently being restructured as an OST-supported committee to enable continuing representation of Scotland, Wales and Northern Ireland. OST has responsibility for ensuring that R&D issues which cross departmental boundaries are effectively handled and that emerging trans-departmental issues are kept under regular review through the Trans-departmental Science and Technology Directorate, in liaison with departmental chief scientists. The recently reconstituted Council for Science and Technology, for which OST provides secretariat support, advises on the philosophy and principles for S&T expenditure[49]. Moreover, a new Ministerial Science Group was established in December 1998, building on the Foresight Ministerial Group set up in October 1997. The purpose of this group of junior ministers is to ensure that their Departments' policies take due account of Government policies on S&T, to steer and promote Foresight across Whitehall and beyond, and to consider implementation of the OST guidelines on the use of scientific advice in Government (OST, 1997, 1998).

6.7   A review of departmental S&T expenditure in 1996, the so-called Boundaries Review, "... did not find major areas of duplication or unnecessary overlap" and concluded that, in general, the co-ordination mechanisms across Government were working well, but that "there is

---

[49] *The CST is currently preparing reports on the S&T activities of the 5 leading R&D spending departments in the UK (Health, Ministry of Agriculture, Fisheries and Food (MAFF), Department of the Environment, Transport and the Regions (DETR), DTI and MoD) with respect to recommendations for rationalisation and co-ordination, on the exploitation of science, and on science in schools (CST, 1999).*

some scope for improving co-ordination and collaboration" (OST/DTI, 1996, preface). The review reported favourably on existing co-ordination mechanisms such as the work of the Foresight Panels in this area, the Concordats between the Departments and the Research Councils[50], and the LINK programme of support for collaborative R&D between industry and the science base. It also noted areas where departmental co-ordination on specific issues was particularly well developed such as, among many others, the National Health Service (NHS) R&D Managers Group, the Agriculture, Food and Fisheries Research Funders Group, the Interdepartmental Group on Public Health, the UK Biodiversity Steering Group, and the Committee on Marine Science and Technology. Noted, however, was the lack of attention to issues of co-ordination in the Forward Look exercise, and the need for more co-ordination in biotechnology, transport and the environment, energy, and information technology.

6.8   DTI's Innovation Policy and Standards Directorate is responsible for administering an Innovation Budget[51] worth some £200m per annum and, working with the Innovation Unit and others, for developing DTI innovation and technology policy. The IU, with its team of Government officials and industrial secondees, works with a range of organisations such as the CBI to promote a culture of innovation in organisations across the UK. The Unit runs the annual Innovation Lecture and produces the UK R&D Scoreboard, the Capex Scoreboard and other material highlighting behavioural issues related to the environment for innovation. The IU industrial secondees also work closely with Regional

---

50   *These Concordats are frameworks for the systematic development, review and evaluation of the respective needs, activities, expectations and obligations of Departments and Research Councils.*

51   *The Innovation Budget is DTI's primary funding stream for innovation support activities. The budget aim is to help the UK improve its innovation performance by supporting a number of activities designed to help firms take advantage of the UK's science and engineering base and new technologies and best practices.*

Development Agencies (RDAs) in developing their regional innovation and technology priorities. A 20 per cent increase in the DTI innovation budget, to complement the increased science budget of the CSR, was a recommendation of the 1998 White Paper on Competitiveness[52]. The White Paper emphasised a changing role for Government in S&T, one that is increasingly in brokering greater collaboration between firms, universities and Government (DTI, 1998). This, the White Paper argued, due to the nature of modern S&T processes, must be co-ordinated at the regional or local level through the DTI and the new RDAs, first proposed in the December 1997 White Paper *Renewing the Regions: Building Partnerships for Prosperity* and formally constituted on 1 April 1999, building on national and European programmes.

6.9   The White Paper focused on the creation and exploitation of knowledge and the development of UK capabilities, with particular emphasis on the more effective exploitation of the science and engineering base and the promotion of partnerships with business to commercialise knowledge and expertise. New activities included both University Challenge, Science Enterprise Challenge, already noted above, as well as a Reach-Out fund to help develop university researchers into entrepreneurs, and, announced later in the DTI's *Expenditure Plans Report 1999/02*, £26m increased funding for the Smart Programme (raising it to £105m over three years) which provides grants to individuals and SMEs to help them research and develop new products and processes. With regard specifically to R&D, the 1998 Budget consultation document *Innovating for the Future: Investing in R&D*, noted: "By itself new technology is no guarantee of success, but in general the Government believes that an increase in R&D activity would be of benefit to the economy" (HM Treasury/DTI, 1998, p.5). Specific initiatives contemplated include improved R&D tax incentives, venture capital for

---

[52]   *DTI's Expenditure Plans Report 1999/02 announced the Government's intention to increase the Innovation Budget over the next three years by more than 20 per cent, rising to £230m by 2002.*

innovation and R&D, and protection of intellectual property. Hence, the 1998 Budget, the CSR, the White Paper on Competitiveness, and the Forward Look all lay great priority on promoting science, innovation and enterprise as a means of achieving the key objectives of improved productivity and sustainable growth and employment in the UK.

European Union

6.10   Funds in the EU are channelled to R&D through the Structural Funds for less developed regions and the Framework Programme of R&D activities, the primary purpose of each being improvement in the competitiveness of European industry. The model for regional R&D and innovation strategy in the EU is Regional Innovation Strategy/Regional Innovation and Technology Transfer Strategy (RIS/RITTS) - a long-term action-based strategy for innovation-led economic development integrated between the public and private sectors and based around SMEs. 100 regions in Europe have either completed or are in the process of completing a RIS/RITTS (Map 1). The last call for proposals on RITTS was December 1997, for projects to begin by December 1998. RIS continues to 2000 under the current round of Structural Funds, and RITTS under the Fifth Framework Programme (FP5) for research. The European regional experience of RIS/RITTS has been confirmed in EU evaluation to have been an important and positive one, leading to new integrated approaches to R&D and innovation strategy. RIS/RITTS has been a tool for regions to increase awareness of innovation, and to raise funding and set priorities for R&D and innovation. The RIS/RITTS projects have emphasised process and have evolved into innovation-led economic development strategies for their regions, based on consensus and public-private partnership.

6.11   As stated in a 1998 European Commission communication, in the next EU initiative regarding regional innovation policy it will be "... necessary to ensure that R&D and innovation actions are integrated within the productive fabric of the regions through development plans" (EC,

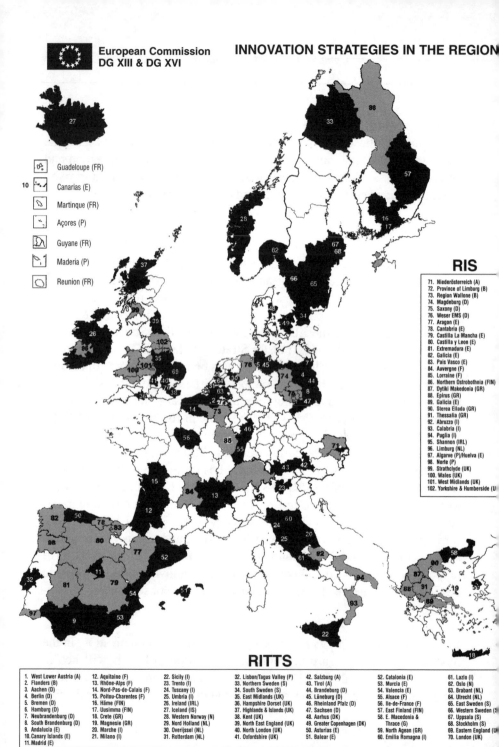

European Commission
DG XIII & DG XVI

INNOVATION STRATEGIES IN THE REGION

Guadeloupe (FR)

Canarias (E)

Martinque (FR)

Açores (P)

Guyane (FR)

Maderia (P)

Reunion (FR)

RIS

71. Niederösterreich (A)
72. Province of Limburg (B)
73. Region Wallone (B)
74. Magdeburg (D)
75. Saxony (D)
76. Weser EMS (D)
77. Aragon (E)
78. Cantabria (E)
79. Castilla La Mancha (E)
80. Castilla y Leon (E)
81. Extremadura (E)
82. Galicia (E)
83. Pais Vasco (E)
84. Auvergne (F)
85. Lorraine (F)
86. Northern Ostrobothnia (FIN)
87. Dytiki Makedonia (GR)
88. Epirus (GR)
89. Galicia (E)
90. Sterea Eilada (GR)
91. Thessalia (GR)
92. Abruzzo (I)
93. Calabria (I)
94. Puglia (I)
95. Shannon (IRL)
96. Limburg (NL)
97. Algarve (P)/Huelva (E)
98. Norte (P)
99. Strathclyde (UK)
100. Wales (UK)
101. West Midlands (UK)
102. Yorkshire & Humberside (U

RITTS

1. West Lower Austria (A)	12. Aquitaine (F)	22. Sicily (I)	32. Lisbon/Tagus Valley (P)	42. Salzburg (A)	52. Catalonia (E)	61. Lazlo (I)
2. Flanders (B)	13. Rhône-Alps (F)	23. Trento (I)	33. Northern Sweden (S)	43. Tirol (A)	53. Murcia (E)	62. Oslo (N)
3. Aachen (D)	14. Nord-Pas-de-Calais (F)	24. Tuscany (I)	34. South Sweden (S)	44. Brandeburg (D)	54. Valencia (E)	63. Brabant (NL)
4. Berlin (D)	15. Poitou-Charentes (F)	25. Umbria (I)	35. East Midlands (UK)	45. Lüneburg (D)	55. Alsace (F)	64. Utrecht (NL)
5. Bremen (D)	16. Häme (FIN)	26. Ireland (IRL)	36. Hampshire Dorset (UK)	46. Rheinland Pfalz (D)	56. Ile-de-France (F)	65. East Sweden (S)
6. Hamburg (D)	17. Uusimma (FIN)	27. Iceland (IS)	37. Highlands & Islands (UK)	47. Sachsen (D)	57. East Finland (FIN)	66. Western Sweden (S
7. Neubrandenburg (D)	18. Crete (GR)	28. Western Norway (N)	38. Kent (UK)	48. Aarhus (DK)	58. E. Macedonia &	67. Uppsala (S)
8. South Brandenburg (D)	19. Magnesie (GR)	29. Nord Holland (NL)	39. North East England (UK)	49. Greater Copenhagen (DK)	Thrace (G)	68. Stockholm (S)
9. Andalucia (E)	20. Marche (I)	30. Overijssel (NL)	40. North London (UK)	50. Asturias (E)	59. North Agean (GR)	69. Eastern England (UK
10. Canary Islands (E)	21. Milano (I)	31. Rotterdam (NL)	41. Oxfordshire (UK)	51. Balear (E)	60. Emilia Romagna (I)	70. London (UK)
11. Madrid (E)						

(some projects subject to contract negoiation)

Source: European Commiss

1998, p.8) and that these development plans should build on the strengths and potential of the region, diversify and improve the knowledge and economic base, and assist in the creation of new firms and jobs. The next regional initiative was forecast in November 1998 to potentially involve new partnerships programmes between EU, national and regional authorities on various levels of action. These include: analysis of regional economic development needs and potential; development of regional economic development strategies in which R&D and innovation are embedded; implementation of agreed regional programmes for R&D and innovation; and creation of streamlined, focused and inclusive regional partnerships to take responsibility for strategic economic development planning, the co-ordination of policy instruments, and the necessary finance to fund strategy and actions[53].

6.12   RIS/RITTS[54] actions are part of the FP5 Innovation/SME work programme. A "Regional Innovation Observatory" (RINNO) will build on the achievements of earlier actions on RIS/RITTS by producing a European Directory of regional public support measures for the promotion of innovation. FP5 will seek to "valorise" the results of RIS/RITTS action to intensify the exchange of good practice rather than initiate new large scale actions. It is possible that the network will be enlarged to include regions not initially involved, transferring experience from RIS/RITTS regions to other regions. Specific action under FP5 is still unclear, but it is likely that further action will not have the RITTS label to avoid confusion or the assumption that funding is still available on a similar basis.

6.13   R&D and innovation initiatives will also be integrated into future

---

[53] *From a video conference presentation by Eileen Armstrong, DG XII, European Commission, to the Training Seminar on Innovation Policy and Strategy for Regional Programmes in European, Barcelona, 11-13 November 1998.*

[54] *RITTS is funded under the Framework Programme and RIS under the Structural Funds.*

Structural Funds. Northern Ireland is currently drafting its Structural Fund Plan around Transitional Objective 1 Funding Status for 2000-2006, a special programme package for 2000-2004, and post-1999 community initiatives. This will result in a new Single Programming Document and Programming Supplement. The Programme will be focused on economic regeneration and diversification of the economy, and on making Northern Ireland a more outward and forward looking region in business and social affairs. One special theme of the Programme will presumably be the knowledge-driven economy, with investment focused on R&D, education and training, and new technology collaboration and networking, especially in and for SMEs.

6.14   FP5 is a 4-year strategic research plan of approximately £10bn, with its two fundamental principles being quality in research and transnational co-operation. The mission of FP5 is to "put European research efforts at the service of the people", and to encourage innovation and competitiveness in Europe along the lines of the First Action Plan for Innovation of 1997, which has the twin objectives of gearing research to innovation and strengthening overall co-ordination (EC, 1997). Compared with its predecessors, FP5 is targeted at clearer objectives and is more responsive to the needs of users of research. It also has a clearer focus on the exploitation of results. Based on its share of EU population, Northern Ireland might expect to receive about £30m over 4 years, 1999-2002, from FP5. Research proposals must involve at least 2 organisations in 2 member states or 1 member state and 1 associate state. First expenditure will be in 1999 with focus not only on economic value added of research relevant to commercial business needs but also beyond the competitiveness of European industry to include quality of life and support for European policy development in areas such as transport, health and the environment. Focus is, however, on research where there are significant advantages which can only be achieved through collaboration at the European level.

Republic of Ireland

6.15   Modern publicly funded R&D strategy in the RoI dates from 1987 when a Minister for Science, Technology and Commerce was created within the Department of Enterprise and Employment (DEE). At the same time an Office of Science and Technology was established to co-ordinate EU Structural and Framework R&D programmes and the corresponding National Operational Plan for Science and Technology. OST took responsibility for the development, promotion and co-ordination of Ireland's R&D and innovation policy. To build research capabilities and infrastructure and to set priorities, EU Structural Funds were used for Programmes in Advanced Technologies (PATs) which established research institutes and centres of excellence in biotechnology, advanced manufacturing, opto-electronics, materials technology, software, telecommunications, and power electronics.

6.16   In 1993-94 the Science, Technology and Innovation Advisory Council (STIAC) Task-force was established to report on S&T. Using the concept of an interdependent "National System of Innovation" involving industry, education and Government, and championed in reports in 1992 and 1993 for the National Economic and Social Council (NESC), the Task Force argued that S&T policy must be co-ordinated at the highest level[55]. It recommended an interdepartmental committee on S&T, an enhanced role for OST, and a permanent council for S&T (see also Kinsella and McBierty, 1995).

6.17   The themes of the STIAC report were reflected in the 1996 White Paper on Science, Technology and Innovation (STI) (DEE, 1996). The White Paper recognised the need for a co-ordinating mechanism at central Government level to ensure efficiency of spending, value for money, and a coherent approach across all S&T spending Departments. It

---

[55]   *See also NESC (1998).*

recommended the establishment of an annual science budget and S&T estimates, a high level interdepartmental committee under the direction of a cabinet committee on S&T, a national foresight programme, and the establishment of a permanent council for S&T. Forfás, the policy advisory and co-ordination board for industrial development and science and technology in the RoI, was given responsibility for the science budget which records all public investment in S&T (Forfás, 1998). Forfás has statutory responsibility in relation to S&T co-ordination and policy advice, including co-ordination of public and private R&D. It carries out many activities on behalf of OST.

6.18   A Task Force was put in charge of implementing the recommendations of the 1996 White Paper.   In 1997 the Inter-Departmental Committee (IDC) for S&T was established, chaired by the Minister for Science, Technology and Commerce, and with representation of the 12 Departments at Assistant Secretary level, to prioritise spending across Departments.   Also in 1997 the permanent Irish Council for Science Technology and Innovation (ICSTI) was established with remit to advise the Minister responsible for S&T, OST, and the Board of Forfás, on policy and strategy for science, technology, innovation and related matters.   Forfás provides secretariat support to ICSTI.   The Task-force also recommended that a full Cabinet Minister for science be established. This resulted in the renaming of the Department of Education and the creation of a Minister for Education and Science.   This Minister bridges the Department of Education and Science and the Department of Enterprise, Trade and Employment, and there are also full Ministers for industry and for education.   A third new and interrelated infrastructure element that was created was a Cabinet Sub-Committee for S&T. Beginning in 1998 the S&T expenditure of each Department was recorded together in an annex to the Government Expenditure Estimates.

6.19   An ICSTI recommendation in 1998 with regard to departmental R&D spending was for the establishment of a Strategic Innovation Investment Fund to be administered by the IDC on S&T (ICSTI, 1998a).

It was proposed that this should be made up of contributions from the Exchequer, from each Department (top-sliced from their S&T vote), and from European funds. Departments would then compete for the consolidated funds, helping to direct expenditure towards changing national priorities. ICSTI argued that, without the establishment of such a fund, R&D expenditures and existing priorities would remain fixed in Department votes, to be rolled over year after year without attention to changing needs. It was envisaged that the fund could grow to be as much as 25 per cent of current departmental R&D spending.

6.20   Technology Foresight Ireland was launched in March 1998 under ICSTI and Forfás and reported in April 1999 (ICSTI, 1999b). It argues for an approximately £500m Technology Foresight Fund over 5 years, with new expenditures directed towards building research capability in priority areas established by Foresight, reflecting long-term priorities rather than short-term needs. The fund would be administered by the Industry Department, and the two major priorities identified were Information and Communication Technology (ICT) and Biotechnology[56].

6.21   Another initiative launched in 1998 was the Science and Technological Innovation (Investment) Fund, an £180m three-year programme for research based on public-private partnership and channelled through the universities and institutes of technology. The programme includes £150m in new capital spending for building laboratories, libraries and computer and research facilities in third-level educational institutions designed to make these institutions centres of excellence in particular disciplines. £75m involves new Government expenditures and tax expenditures (£25m in tax relief for corporate investors) matched by £75m in private sector funding to be raised by the higher education institutions. The programme also includes £30m in

---

[56] *Since 1987 the Government has in fact funded a major PAT, BioResearch Ireland (BRI), in the biotechnology field, which has successfully commercialised some of its R&D, and interacts with industry.*

current spending on grants, scholarships and salaries for scientific and other research, 75 per cent of which will come from the public sector. A significant factor in the scheme is that the allocation of funds is to the Department of Education and Science and not to the existing major funder of scientific research, the Department of Enterprise, Trade and Employment[57]. Applications can only be made to the funds by third-level educational institutions, with or without private sector partners, on the basis of presentation of, and adherence to, their strategic plans for research[58].

6.22   ICSTI continues to be active in making recommendations for change. The S&T expenditures of Government departments are still felt by ICSTI to be somewhat ad hoc and a weak focus on S&T across and within departments is noted. The attention to R&D in the public sector and in universities in the RoI still lags far behind other EU and OECD countries, and the R&D and innovation system relies heavily on the private business sector, especially multinational corporation inward investors. Total R&D spending has risen from 0.85 per cent of GDP in 1989 to almost 1.5 per cent in 1997, but it is R&D in the business sector that has fully accounted for this increase, rising from 0.5 per cent of GDP in 1989 to 1.11 per cent in 1997. The proportion of total R&D financed by Government is just 23 per cent, involving an expenditure of 0.11 per cent of GDP in Government Departments and 0.27 per cent of GDP in the higher education sector (ICSTI, 1999a). These latter figures are well

---

[57]   *However, the Minister for Education and Science will consult with the Minister for Industry.*

[58]   *The rationale for the scheme was put succinctly by the Minister for Education and Science, Mr Martin who stated "you cannot have a cutting-edge economy without cutting-edge research" (Irish Times, 20 November 1998). The chairman of the Higher Education Authority, Dr Don Thornhill, said the programme gives researchers the chance to create "world class research in world class conditions" (Irish Times, 20 November 1998).*

below EU averages[59].

6.23   ICSTI has recently called for a target total R&D expenditure of 2.5 per cent of GDP, with an increased and strategic commitment of the public sector, and a strategic management approach to the overall S&T budget. The Council stated "... the low level of research performed by the public sector in support of its strategic objectives [is] a weakness in the Irish innovation system" (ICSTI, 1998b, p.20), but also that "... in deciding the balance of investment ... there should be a strong emphasis on building up the performance, capability and skills of the business sector in terms of R&D and innovation and in promoting industry/institution collaboration" (ICSTI, 1999a, p.36).   Regarding departmental R&D spending, ICSTI has recommended, in addition to increased spending and commitment, a rolling three-year national R&D plan, to be taken into account in allocating funds to Departments, based on national social and economic development needs.   Funding to each Department, it recommends, should be based on an open competitive process, with evaluation and monitoring as for impact and the meeting of objectives.   The IDC on S&T would allocate funds and establish the national plan, which would be published and debated.   ICSTI also recommends that each of the 12 Departments appoint their own scientific advisors[60].   Such changes are seen as necessary to move the public support system for R&D and S&T in the RoI much closer to the UK system, which in general is viewed favourably.

6.24   In regard to public funding of R&D in industry and education, rather than public sector R&D activity, the current system in the RoI is split between the Department of Enterprise, Trade and Employment, which funds developmental applied research (through, for example, R&D

---

[59]   *See Section 5 above.*

[60]   *Current public sector R&D performance is heavily weighted towards Agricultural and Marine research, together accounting for almost 60 per cent of all activity.*

grants to companies) and the Department of Education and Science, which funds basic and strategic research. ICSTI recommends some reform to the industry R&D grants scheme (the Industry Operational Programme "Measure 1") with more emphasis on building long-term capability in firms rather than on short-term subsidy, on encouraging new R&D performers, and on focusing on companies with credible long-term development plans based on R&D and innovation. With regard to the funding of basic and strategic research, the National Research Support Fund Board was established in 1995 to fund, through Enterprise Ireland, strategic research in higher education, based on grants for projects. This now complements the basic block funding for research of the Department of Education. It is generally agreed in the RoI that there needs to be increased resources allocated to the building up of public R&D infrastructure, in order that it can complement growing business spending on R&D. ICSTI is recommending that for this purpose, and to help in developing the national system of innovation holistically, all R&D measures under the National Development Plan and EU Structural Funds should be brought together under a single programme of R&D funding under the joint direction of the Enterprise, Trade and Employment and Education and Science Departments. A single mechanism to fund R&D would reduce the number of separate measures and would be a streamlined and focused approach, better able to respond to the priorities of Technology Foresight Ireland and other initiatives.

6.25   The recent recommendations of ICSTI have been endorsed by the Economic and Social Research Institute (ESRI) in its advice to Government on priorities for the national investment programme 2000-2006. The ESRI researchers state: "The case for support of R&D is extremely strong since it has very significant potential returns on investment. Current levels of public investment in R&D in Ireland are low by international standards. We recommend a substantial increase in public expenditure on R&D in the next decade" (Fitz Gerald et al, 1999, p.279), and: "We recommend that genuine public good research should grow by substantially more than the overall total" (p.219) but that "The challenge for policy makers is to devise suitable targeting devices to channel resources to the true public good activities within R&D" (p.61). The ESRI researchers' targets for public R&D spending are, however, more conservative than those of ICSTI. They recommend targeting R&D as a percentage of GDP at its current level, which still, however, involves substantial real increases in public and private R&D spending, given projected growth in real GDP. The ESRI researchers endorse the notion of a single programme for publicly funded R&D, but argue that R&D to underpin policy making should remain within the Departments and within the remit of the IDC, and not be part of the single fund. But the single fund, they argue, would help in establishing transparent mechanisms for the allocation of public resources to R&D, and ensure their maximum effectiveness in striking the correct balance between basic/strategic research and research supportive of private firms.

Regional and National Case Studies

Scotland

6.26   In Scotland around £250m on R&D spending is controlled by the Scottish Administration with a recognition that the present system of co-ordination and collaboration in regional R&D is sub-optimal. The way forward is currently under debate. Discussion is focusing not on institutions (whether there is a need for a Scottish OST or CST) but on the process by which R&D strategy in Scotland can be taken forward. Under devolution, this is the responsibility of the Minister for Science and Education. The main Departments and other strategic partners in the Scottish publicly funded R&D system, as it currently exists, are:

- The Scottish Office Education and Industry Department (SOEID), to be split under devolution, which runs the S&T unit and is responsible for funding the 22 HEIs, involving approximately £120m in expenditure.

- The Scottish Office Agriculture, Environment and Fisheries Department (SOAEFD) which administers approximately £70m in expenditure, involving funding for the Scottish Agricultural and Biological Research Centres (SABRIs), which are similar to and co-ordinated with the major research Councils in the UK (the Biotechnology and Biological Sciences Research Council (BBSRC) and the Natural Environment Research Council (NERC)). The Department also funds the Scottish Agricultural College which is engaged in research, teaching and advisory services, and the Scottish Agricultural Science Agency (SASA). The Department recently published its *Strategy for Agricultural, Biological and Related Research 1998-2003*.

- The Scottish Office Department of Health (SODoH) Chief Scientist Office (CSO) with a £40m Research Strategy for the NHS in Scotland. This is co-ordinated through a Central Research Unit which administers policy-related research and grants to researchers. An R&D Strategy for the NHS in Scotland was published in July 1998, updating the first strategy published in 1993, as was a Technology Audit of the NHS in Scotland (CSO/SODoH, 1998).

- Scottish Enterprise, an economic powerhouse agency involved in the commercialisation of Government and university research within a cluster strategy, focused on four priority areas; oil and gas, food, electronics and biotechnology. Government research in agriculture and health is also included.

6.27 An initiative begun in 1995 by Scottish Enterprise and the Royal Society of Edinburgh, the Technology Ventures Initiative (TVI), closely linked to the UK's Foresight programme, is concerned with the poor rate of Scottish commercialisation of Scottish research - that the outstanding science base in Scotland (with 9 per cent of the UK population but 15 per cent of the UK academic science base) is producing S&T results which are largely commercialised outside Scotland (Scottish Enterprise, 1996). TVI is designed to break down barriers between the academic, Government and business communities in Scotland and create a well networked high technology community. An example of what can be achieved is perhaps that of the University of Strathclyde, cited by the UK Cabinet Office on S&T as being one of the two most successful universities in the UK in working with industry and in developing academic research with commercial application. Another Scottish initiative is the Glasgow Science Park, a £70m millennium project, which aims to propel Glasgow into the position of third-ranked science city in the UK. In addition, the Strathclyde region is carrying out a RIS project, and is a member of the Industrial Regions group of RIS/RITTS, alongside other regions such as Yorkshire and Humberside and the West Midlands. A RITTS project was also carried out by the Highlands and Islands region. The Royal Society of Edinburgh is an independent body that provides advice to Government on S&T policy.

6.28   A Knowledge Economy Task Force, chaired by the Business and Industry Minister, and inclusive of Higher Education Institution (HEI) principals, the Scottish Higher Education Funding Council (SHEFC), and Scottish Enterprise, submitted its report *Scotland: Towards the Knowledge Economy* (Scottish Office, 1999) to the Science and Education Minister in April 1999. This calls for an integrated Research Strategy for Scotland, between Government Departments, universities, economic development agencies, and the business community, involving a refocusing of funds and new funding mechanisms making use of Foresight. Initiatives proposed over the next 3 years include a £7m boost for strategic facilities for the commercialisation of research in universities and colleges through SHEFC, and £11m (through University Challenge) for Scottish Enterprise to align academic research within their cluster strategy, bringing companies to the universities. This involves additional resources for the commercialisation of research through spin-out companies (ie companies formed as a result of university research), the formation of institutes and commercial subsidiaries, and new incentives for university staff to engage in commercialisation of their R&D. Also included are proposals for a Centre for Science and Enterprise in Scotland under the UK's Science Enterprise Challenge, building on the Entrepreneurial Education Initiative that was initiated in 1994. The SHEFC's Research Development Grant Scheme, with a budget of £10m, also has the objective of guiding research capability in the universities to the needs of society and the Scottish economy. Economic development strategy in Scotland is thus evolving around a knowledge-led approach, integrating the work of the Scottish Enterprise cluster teams with the science base in universities and research institutes in order to maximise the economic benefit to Scotland of the overall Scottish R&D effort.

Wales

6.29   Wales provides an example of a publicly funded regional R&D innovation and economic development strategy spearheaded by an economic development agency, in this case, the Welsh Development Agency (WDA). In the early 1990s the WDA initiated a Regional Technology Plan (RTP), one of the first European regions to do so (WDA, 1998)[61]. The work of the RTP was carried forward by the Technology Transfer Group of WDA, which has championed the creation of Technology Forums (or Clubs) in key industrial sectors (such as automotive and electronics, medical technology, opto-electronics, mechatronics, materials technology, printing and coating and pest management), led a Centre of Expertise Programme with the universities, and now produces outstanding S&T periodicals such as Technology Wales and Advances Wales. The WDA also publishes Research Wales, a directory of all researchers in Welsh universities and areas of specialisation and Interlab, a directory of research laboratories, and other sectoral directories of company and academic research.

---

[61]   *This evolved into the current RIS/RITTS programme of the EU discussed above. The original idea behind the EU programme came from Wales.*

6.30   The RTP has resulted in the mainstreaming of R&D, S&T and innovation strategy into economic strategy in Wales, as exemplified by the economic strategy consultation paper *Pathway to Prosperity - A New Economic Agenda for Wales* of July 1998 and the consultation document on a Know How Centre for Wales. S&T and innovation issues are placed at the top of the political agenda, and fully embedded into regional competitiveness strategy. Recent initiatives include investment in Know How Wales, with a particular emphasis on SMEs, which links industry with Welsh universities and technology institutes, and a new Technology and Innovation Group as part of a new economic powerhouse WDA. S&T and innovation will be incorporated as horizontal themes into future EU Structural Programmes for Wales, further helping to embed the culture of innovation. Academic-industry links have been stimulated by the strategic approach taken in the RTP and Business Connect Wales and the creation of the Technology Forums. The RTP has helped to stimulate the demand for R&D among SMEs and to integrate R&D and innovation. The overall coherence of the approach to regional R&D and innovation has led to the mainstreaming of R&D and innovation policy into partnership-based and knowledge-led economic development strategy and Structural Funds programmes. Initiatives include developing an Entrepreneurship Plan along the lines of the RTP, to further instil the culture of innovation.

North East England

6.31   The new RDA for the North East of England (One NorthEast) has the remit for S&T and R&D strategy. A specific responsibility of the RDA, as with the other RDAs in GB, is "the preparation of Regional Innovation Strategies, integrating them with their economic strategies to promote innovation and the transfer of physical and managerial technologies and techniques from universities and research centres, and from progressive firms, into the wider business community" (RIS/Yorkshire and the Humber, 1999, p.21). There are a number of blocks already in place for the RDA in the North East to build upon. A

Regional Innovation and Technology Strategy (RITS) - which served as the North East RIS - was carried out in the period 1997-99. An EU-funded competitiveness project was carried out in 1996-1998, which bench-marked regional economic performance, with a vision for the North East "to become the fastest changing region in Europe, where enterprise is systemic and competitiveness is self-sustaining"[62].

6.32   There are five universities in the region with particular strengths in engineering, life sciences, chemicals and ICTs. For many years they have worked together on the Higher Education Support for Industry in the North (HESIN) initiative. In 1999 HESIN was re-formatted into a new body, Universities for the North East (UNE). UNE has among its aims closer inter-university collaboration to re-package high-powered academic R&D for commercialisation by regional firms, especially SMEs. Another regional HEI partnership, Knowledge House (which provides a common gateway for business to HEI expertise) was commended as an exemplar project in the Dearing Report on Higher Education in the UK (NCIHE, 1997). The project is to be extended beyond its current S&T focus to embrace a wider brief, including enterprise and entrepreneurship issues.

6.33   The universities are also members of North East Technology Support (NETS). NETS is a partnership of 24 key providers of technology services to industry in the North East. It comprises HEIs, FE colleges and independent organisations. As well as providing a mechanism for co-ordinating the region's technology support infrastructure it facilitates access to practical help for companies. Day to day management of the partnership is carried out by the Regional Technology Centre (RTC). RTC also hosts the UNE and Knowledge House co-ordinators, the Relay Centre (which promotes EU R&D

---

[62] *Ten per cent of the top spending R&D companies in the UK have facilities in the North East including Zeneca, Du Pont, Cummins, British Steel, Proctor and Gamble, and Sun Microsystems.*

activities) and the regional co-ordinator for the Foresight programme.

Yorkshire and Humberside

6.34   In response to a need to transform from a dependence on old industries such as steel, textiles, shipbuilding and mechanical engineering, but with an isolated and fragmented high technology community spread over 9 universities and an industrial R&D effort that was weak by national standards, the Yorkshire and Humberside region initiated a RIS project in 1996. It is based on a sectoral strategy, with 11 business-led sector working groups, involving sectors such as chemicals, medical technology, food and textiles and clothing, and also issues of all-sector support, such as links with higher and further education, stimulating new company growth, and implications of the information society. Major initiatives such as Medilink in medical technology have emerged as outputs, as have regional innovation forums and regular newsletters[63].

6.35   The RDA for Yorkshire and Humberside (Yorkshire Forward) was established on 1 April 1999. It already has at its disposal the help of the Yorkshire and Humberside University Association (YHUA) set up in

---

[63]   *At the Innovation Forum held in April 1998, John Battle MP, then Minister for Science, Energy and Industry, commented, "RIS is this region's opportunity to put down firm foundations for the building of a vibrant and profitable business structure. To establish a climate of successful exploitation of ideas, increased creativity, a "can-do, no-blame" culture, and a world class trained workforce. I welcome the fact that business, through the RIS sector networks, have put aside any differences and turf wars in the sure conviction that partnership and co-operation will be beneficial". At the Innovation Forum held in November 1998, Richard Caborn, Minister for the Regions, Regeneration and Planning, noted, "The Innovation Strategy will play a major part in the Regional Development Agency, ... what you have been doing in Yorkshire and the Humber is going to give some real added value by making a more intelligent assessment of what your region needs and delivering that through partnership with the business community. I think that what Yorkshire has done in its development of an Innovation Strategy is by far the best I have seen in the country" (RIS/Yorkshire and the Humber, 1999).*

1993 and the Regional Research Observatory, set up in 1989. The YHUA operates through four working groups, one devoted to encouraging regional economic development, and the others to ensuring collaboration between the nine universities (Bennesworth, 1999). It participates fully in the Yorkshire and Humberside RIS project.

South Sweden

6.36   South Sweden, with a population of 1.35m, is an example of a region approximately the same economic size as Northern Ireland and similarly transforming from such industries as heavy engineering and shipbuilding into high technology. The region contains the University of Lund, the Lund Institute of Technology, the Swedish University of Agricultural Sciences and the Swedish Institute for Food Research, and of total employment of 539,000 in the region, 6,500 personnel are in R&D. The town of Lund is ringed with research parks and large high technology corporations. R&D in large corporations in Sweden is extremely strong, but a regional weakness in South Sweden was in R&D in SMEs. This has been addressed by a RITTS and a Knowledge Bridge between universities, colleges and SMEs, both managed by Teknopol AB. Teknopol is an organisation that describes itself as an intermediary between SMEs and the world of research, and was formed in 1995 with funds distributed from a labour fund, the Technology Bridge Foundation. It finds commercial uses for research results from the University of Lund and is a 'One Stop Shop' for SMEs for innovation and technology. Projects managed by Teknopol include the RITTS (jointly with Lund University and the Regional Council), Teknoseed, a £5m venture capital fund, Forskerpatent Syd AB, an intellectual property rights initiative, and Kundapsbron, the Knowledge Bridge.

6.37   One outcome of the RITTS was that university liaison offices were reorganised, another that the Regional Council devised an innovation strategy, and another that the Knowledge Bridge was set up. Teknopol runs and staffs all liaison offices in each university and college in the region, forming a large network of support. Companies approach their municipal Government contacts for R&D support, who put them onto the Knowledge Bridge regional director and project leaders. Some funding is provided by the Swedish National Board for Industrial and Technological Development (NUTEK). A new cross-border high technology environment to unite universities and industry is the Oresund University initiative linking universities and colleges on both sides of the Oresund, concurrent with construction of the fixed link Oresund Bridge between Copenhagen and Malmo.

Denmark

6.38   Denmark, with a population of 5.5m, provides an example of best practice in national R&D strategy. The system of publicly funded R&D is based around 7 research councils and 40 or so Technological Service Institutes. 15 of these are in the Advanced Technology Group, of which the Danish Technological Institute is a major one, with 6 centres around the country. These institutes form a Council of Institutes and are private not-for-profit polytechnological service foundations with about 15 per cent of their revenue from the state. Most SMEs have some contact and collaboration with at least one institute[64]. The principle of support for R&D in Denmark is not grants but four-year 'centre contracts' between Government and the Institutes for work performed, a new system that began in 1995. These contracts between Government, universities, businesses and institutes involve R&D training, technology transfer, and expertise building. The political body overseeing the system is the Council of Technical Service, an agency of the Ministry of Industry. The Danish Technological Institute promotes regional R&D co-operation projects (each involving businesses and at least 2 public institutions), and

---

[64]   *Two initiatives in this regard are the Icebreaker system, with Government funding SMEs 50 per cent of the salary of hiring their first engineer or scientist, and the Introductory Discount System (DISCO) to encourage SMEs to sign R&D contracts with Institutes as a stepping stone to bigger innovations.*

universities have their own R&D and technology transfer initiatives. The Government also has a four year renewable centre contract with the National Laboratory. There are also 15 Technological Information Centres spatially distributed across Denmark, financed by the Danish Ministry of Industry. These are independent, not-for-profit centres that offer consultancy services free of charge to SMEs. An example at the regional level is the Institute for Production Technology at Odense University, which has managed, with the help of IT, to reinvent the shipbuilding process at Odense Steel Shipyard Ltd.

6.39   Five years ago a national strategy for R&D in Denmark was devised - more interventionist, with R&D a high priority and with an R&D target of 2 per cent of GDP spend, focusing on useability, commercialisation, infrastructure support and R&D training. Priorities are set indicatively via Foresight. The Ministry of Research and Information Technology was established in 1993, spinning off from the Ministry of Education and Science. This partly directs university funding, with universities not as free as previously in setting their own agendas, and with the publication of their research plans as the basis for funding. One of the largest research institutions in Denmark is the Danish Institute of Agricultural Science, established in 1997 by amalgamating four separate centres, and funded by the Ministry of Food, Agriculture and Fisheries.

6.40   The Ministry of Research in Denmark co-ordinates research across all Government ministries through an Inter-Ministerial Group and steers a research plan with annual priority setting. The four-year contract basis of research allows for competition between research councils, research institutes, and the universities, and makes sure that publicly funded R&D in Denmark does not become ossified in non-discretionary annual appropriations.

The Netherlands

6.41   R&D expenditure exceeds 2 per cent of GDP in The Netherlands with strong home-based multinationals such as Phillips, Shell and Unilever benefiting from tax credits for R&D[65]. With regard to publicly funded R&D, there is an Advisory Council on Science and Technology Policy (AWT) established in 1990, and reconstituted in 1997, with additional responsibilities for co-ordinating Technology Foresight, with a research staff and secretariat. There are two ministries involved in R&D co-ordination at the national level: the Ministry of Education, Culture and Science (science policy) and the Ministry of Economic Affairs (industry and technology policy). The former manages a Science Directorate to co-ordinate research across all ministries and produces an annual science budget, and the latter administers a £250m fund to stimulate R&D, one-third as grants to industry, and the rest to research institutes and to industry/university collaboration. A Ministerial Committee also sits at Cabinet level, with the Prime Minister as Chair, on Science, Technology and Information Policy. The Chairman of AWT sits on this committee in a non-voting advisory capacity. Foresight Panels exist to give clear direction to the system.

6.42   The Ministry of Traffic and Infrastructure, Department of Agriculture, Department of Health, and Ministry of Education and Science all have research laboratories, but some divisions have been privatised or merged with research institutes under restructuring. The Netherlands Organisation for Applied Research (TNO), is a system of research institutes set up in the 1930s, originally financed by Government but now through public-private partnership and employing 4,000 R&D personnel. Institutes each specialise, but all compete for money from Government and the private sector. TNO does research for a number of

---

65   *The Randstad region of 7.2m encompassing Noord Holland, Zuid Holland, Utrecht and Flevoland (and the cities of Amsterdam, The Hague and Rotterdam) is one of the most densely populated areas of Europe, in a nation of 15m population.*

Ministries. An Inter-Departmental Committee decides what TNOs should do for each Ministry over four-year cycles. Four Technological Top Institutes, with special remit to meet the needs of industry, are in food, chemicals, telematics and new materials. The Ministry of Economic Affairs encourages co-operation between universities, business and Governments. In regard to the universities, the Agricultural University of Wageningen is funded by the Ministry of Agriculture, Nature Conservation and Fisheries. A process is in place to increase the autonomy of the universities, to enhance efficiency and effectiveness and allow differentiation. SMEs are loath to go to universities, but go to the TNOs and the Vocational Institutes of Technology and Business instead. However, SYNTENS is a network of 15 regional innovation centres for SMEs funded by the central Government in which universities also collaborate. RIS/RITTS projects have been undertaken by the Overijssel, Noord Holland, Rotterdam, Brabant and Utrecht regions.

Conclusion

6.43   These descriptions of policy practices in regard to publicly funded R&D elsewhere are intended to suggest policy innovations that might be considered for Northern Ireland, although of course Northern Ireland must forge its own approach to knowledge-led regional economic development in the context of its own unique institutions, culture and economic structure. However, what lessons can Northern Ireland learn from these other regions and nations, in regard to overcoming problems in their publicly funded R&D systems and in forging better strategies, and can Northern Ireland do the same using similar approaches? The regional models discussed in this section are all in some way appropriate to a discussion of publicly funded R&D in Northern Ireland. The UK and EU frameworks are, of course, obviously pertinent to the discussion, as is the RoI's evolving approach. Northern Ireland might also learn from the other regional and national cases examined above, among others.

6.44   The following are some of the institutional mechanisms being used in the regions examined above to improve the efficiency and effectiveness of the public R&D spend, to co-ordinate it within the overall R&D system, and to mesh it with innovation and with the needs of economic development and competitiveness:

- Ministers for Research, S&T, IT - UK, RoI, Denmark.

- Offices or Directorates for S&T - UK, RoI, The Netherlands.

- Foresight - UK, RoI, The Netherlands, Denmark.

- Inter-Departmental S&T Committees - UK, RoI, Denmark, The Netherlands.

- Ministerial and Cabinet S&T Committees - UK, RoI, Denmark, The Netherlands.

- Advisory Councils for S&T - UK, RoI, Scotland, The Netherlands.

- RTPs, RIS/RITTS - Wales, Strathclyde, North East England, Yorkshire and Humberside, South Sweden, The Netherlands regions.

- Targets for increased R&D expenditure - RoI, Denmark.

- Science Budgets - RoI, The Netherlands, UK.

- Single Programmes for R&D funding - RoI (proposed).

- Overall R&D Strategies - RoI, Scotland, The Netherlands, Denmark, Wales.

- Commercialisation Initiatives - Scotland, North East England, South Sweden, Wales.

- RDAs, Economic Development Agencies - North East England, Yorkshire and Humberside, Wales, Scotland.

- Sector-Based Technology Forums, Panels or Clubs - UK, Wales, Yorkshire and Humberside, Scotland.

- Embedding R&D and Innovation Strategy into Regional Economic Development Strategy - Wales, UK RDA regions.

- Knowledge Bridges and Houses - Wales, North East England, South Sweden.

- Limited Term Contract Basis of R&D - Denmark, RoI (proposed).

6.45 Four common themes can be found in these other regions and nations with respect to publicly funded R&D;

- high policy priority given by Government to public and private R&D, S&T and innovation;

- centralised institutions to implement and monitor this policy priority;

- mechanisms and institutions to ensure that the public R&D spend is continuously revised in response to changing priorities; and,

- full embedding of R&D policy into innovation, economic development and competitiveness strategy.

The stress given to these themes has resulted in public-private partnerships in R&D based on co-funding, pump-priming and consensual strategies for R&D and innovation, all helping to raise R&D, innovation and economic performance. Notwithstanding the common institutions and themes found in these other regions, the regions also present differing models and approaches to R&D and innovation. Models have been developed that are appropriate to specific regional profiles; it is useful to consider the different models suggested before we go on to categorise and evaluate the Northern Ireland model in the next sections and suggest ways forward for Northern Ireland in Section 9.

Public-Private Balance

6.46 The UK, Denmark and the Netherlands provide examples of balanced R&D and innovation strategies spearheaded by Ministerial units of Government and mainstreamed into knowledge-led economic development strategies. These nations are seeking a balance between private and public R&D, with partnership between strong R&D capabilities in business, Government, universities and research institutes and guided by Foresight. In the RoI, the model has been unbalanced, based on private sector R&D and innovation strength in foreign-owned multinational corporations and on building linkages from them. However, the RoI is seeking to move closer to the balanced UK and Danish models, by building up public sector R&D capability in universities, colleges and research institutes and co-ordinating a national system of R&D and innovation built around longer-term strategic planning such as Technology Foresight Ireland.

Mission and Diffusion Balance

6.47   Scotland, Wales, North East England, Yorkshire and Humberside and South Sweden provide other models which have, to varying degrees, utilised EU expertise in balancing mission-oriented research through Framework programmes with diffusion-oriented Structural programmes involving SMEs through RIS/RITTS initiatives[66]. In Scotland, the imbalance in public and private research capability is opposite to that of the RoI: public sector mission capabilities are strong in Government and the universities, and strategy has focused on diffusion and commercialisation of public sector research from the strong science base. Moreover, an explicit cluster development and management strategy is being followed in Scotland, building up public and private sector R&D and innovation links. In Wales, the model has been closer to that of the RoI; building on linkages from private sector led R&D through foreign direct investment. However, since the development of the Wales RTP, attention has focused on strengthening industry-academic links in a

---

66   *Mission-oriented R&D involves "Big Science" basic and strategic applied programmes. Diffusion-oriented research lies at the developmental end of the R&D spectrum towards technology transfer to industry.*

sectoral strategy, now evolving into a hybrid cluster-sectoral approach, fully embedded in regional economic development strategy. Yorkshire and Humberside are following a more explicit sector-based strategy, but again heavily oriented to industry-academic links through diffusion. The strategies in North East England and in South Sweden are also based on industry-academic links, but more explicitly through Knowledge Houses and Bridges, based on diffusion of academic R&D and commercial exploitation by local SMEs.

7   THE PUBLICLY FUNDED R&D SYSTEM IN NORTHERN IRELAND

Introduction

7.1   Before considering whether any institutional and strategic innovations with respect to R&D policy are required in Northern Ireland, this section describes the Northern Ireland publicly funded R&D system as it currently exists, according to the major constituent themes, channels of influence and policy, and programmes in the public spend, namely:

- Overall Co-ordination, Networking and Linkages.

- Grants and Assistance to R&D.

- Intramural Department expenditure.

- The Health R&D Programme.

- The University R&D Programme.

ONS estimated that R&D expenditure by Northern Ireland Departments in 1996-97 was £22.8m, net of receipts (Table 7.1 and Figure 4D above). This expenditure includes grants and assistance to R&D (from DED) and of intramural Department expenditure (in the Department of Agriculture for Northern Ireland (DANI), DENI, the Department of the Environment for Northern Ireland (DoE (NI), the Department of Finance and Personnel (DFP) and DHSS). ONS began, in its Government figures, to account for the programme in the health sector in 1997-98, involving an additional £12.7m in expenditure, bringing the estimated total commitment net of receipts in 1997-98 up to £35m (Table 7.1 and Figure 4E in Section 4). The university programme's net addition of £44m of publicly funded research activity in 1996 (Tables 4.3 and 4.4 in Section 4) brought the total public funding commitment in 1996 up to £79m or approximately 52 per cent of total civil R&D in Northern Ireland of £152m (Figure 4F in Section 4). Overall co-ordination, networking and linkages completed the publicly funded R&D system.

93

TABLE 7.1

**R&D Expenditure of Northern Ireland Departments, 1995-96 to 1997-98,
Net of Receipts, Current £**

	1995-96 £m	1996-97 £m	1997-98[1] £m
DANI	8.7	8.0	8.0
DED	10.7	11.4	11.0
DENI	0.3	0.3	0.0
DoE (NI)	0.8	0.8	1.0
DFP	1.4	1.2	1.0
DHSS	2.2	1.3	14.0[2]
Total	24.1	22.8	35.0

[1] *Estimated outturn.*

[2] *Includes expenditure by NDPBs in 1997-98.*

Source: DTI/ONS (1998, Table 1, p.103)

7.2   The sub-sections that follow describe the existing programmes in the public commitment to R&D in Northern Ireland. The next sub-section discusses overall co-ordination and examines what networking and linkages initiatives there are such as Foresight and proposals for a Northern Ireland Science Park. The following sub-sections then discuss, in turn, DED expenditure on grants and assistance to R&D projects, the intramural programme (DANI, DoE (NI), and DFP), the health programme (DHSS and HPSS), and the university programme (through DENI). We conclude with an overall characterisation of the existing R&D system relative to models in comparator regions discussed in Section 6 above. The reader who wishes to avoid detailed discussion of the various programmes in Northern Ireland can read the next section on overall co-ordination, networking and linkages and then skip to the conclusion of the section without loss of continuity.

Overall Co-ordination, Networking and Linkages

7.3   There does not appear to be any formal accounting, monitoring and co-ordination between expenditures in the overall publicly funded R&D programme in Northern Ireland, to the extent that can be found, for example, in some of the other regions discussed in Section 6 above. Thus, the potential for major gaps, overlaps and duplications exists[67]. DED and, in particular, its agency, IRTU, established in 1992, are the authorities charged with the responsibility for overall R&D strategy in Northern Ireland, in collaboration with other relevant bodies such as universities and industry.   The mission of IRTU, as set out in its Corporate Plan, is:

> To provide the leadership, co-ordination and support needed to enhance the contribution of science, engineering and technology to the competitiveness and sustainable development of the economy of Northern Ireland (IRTU, 1998, p.19).

IRTU was established to carry through the DED R&D and innovation strategy, *Innovation 2000* (DED, 1992). With regard to the question of co-ordination, this strategy argued that given the small size of economic institutions in Northern Ireland, collaborative group approaches to R&D are needed, with collective effect, cross-fertilisation of ideas, interdisciplinary exchanges and technology transfer between industry and commerce, universities and other academic and research interests, and Government.

---

67   *Of course, Northern Ireland expenditures fall under the purview of the UK OST and CST, Foresight, Forward Look, EASO, EA and PX (Section 6).*

7.4   One of the operating principles of IRTU as elucidated in its Corporate Plan is to place "much importance on working in partnership with the private sector, universities and other Government departments to attain mutual goals" (IRTU, 1998, p.30). An objective of IRTU is to "Increase the strength of the science and technology base in Northern Ireland and the linkages and networking both among its key players and externally with international counterparts" (IRTU, 1998, p.19). However, the mission, and these principles and objectives of IRTU, are not fully realised. The intramural expenditures of the Departments are not co-ordinated through IRTU, and there is no formal Inter-Departmental R&D Committee. IRTU does not account for nor oversee an overall R&D Budget, but only grants and assistance largely for private sector R&D, which is less than one-third of total Government expenditure. The Government Department, health and university programmes remain largely free of IRTU co-ordination. Moreover, IRTU does not undertake a full accounting and monitoring of all publicly funded R&D activity, in relation to private R&D.

7.5   There does, however, exist some co-ordination, networking and linkages in the R&D system. The Northern Ireland Foresight Programme was established in 1995 under the auspices of IRTU and the Northern Ireland Growth Challenge (NIGC) to ensure that Northern Ireland plays a full part in the UK Foresight initiative. Foresight aims to identify opportunities in the most promising markets and technologies of the future, provide strategic direction to R&D spending, and to forge closer links between Government, business, and academic research. The Northern Ireland Foresight Programme has strengthened Government-business-university R&D links through its sectoral Technology Partnership panels (NIGC, 1995)[68]. Notable outcomes in this regard are the Life and Health Technologies Directorate, the Northern Ireland Food and Drink Association, the Northern Ireland Software Industry Federation

---

[68]   *Since 1996 NIGC has received in excess of £2m of public funds. None of these funds are included in our publicly-funded R&D estimates, since NIGC does not fund R&D.*

(SIF), and the partnership panel in tradable business services. The NIGC emphasis is on assisting networks of firms, working and co-operating together, rather than individual firms, and has undertaken tasks such as bench-marking best practice, developing stronger supplier chains in conjunction with IDB and strengthening linkages between business, universities and research institutions.

7.6   The Chancellor's Economic Package announced in May 1998 contained a major initiative for publicly funded R&D in Northern Ireland that will help in co-ordination and collaboration - £10m for the costs of a Science Park, Northern Ireland participation in the UK £50m University Challenge Fund (UCF), under which UU and QUB can provide venture capital to spin-out and spin-in enterprises (a 'spin-in' enterprise is one which is attracted to the commercial possibilities of university research), and £3m in a special Northern Ireland R&D Challenge Fund to provide venture capital to meet the funding gaps faced by innovating firms at the Science Park and elsewhere (NIEC, 1998). The £10m of public funding for the costs of the Science Park is a substantial contribution to what is envisaged to be a £30m investment, with the balance of funds to be raised by the industry and university partners. The Science Park is envisaged as a distributed network involving the two universities, local councils, economic development agencies, the private sector and venture capitalists, with the main site in Belfast and other sites in Coleraine and Londonderry, with special emphasis on life and health technologies, engineering and IT, and on commercialisation of public and private R&D.

7.7   In March 1999 QUB and UU received £2m from the University Challenge Fund. This will be used in conjunction with £0.5m from QUB and £0.25m from UU to fund technology transfer through UCF (NI) Ltd, focusing on the best science and entrepreneurial staff in both universities and enabling larger and less conservative high technology investments. These are intended to complement the commercial spin-outs of Queen's University Business and Industrial Services (QUBIS) and UUTECH, capitalise on the research strengths of the universities (QUB in engineering and physics and UU in biomedical sciences and informatics), and make more funds available for the allocation of intellectual property rights. Another initiative is the Higher Education Reach Out to Business and the Community Fund. This is designed "to reward and encourage HEIs [higher education institutions] to enhance their interaction with business" (HEFCE, 1999, p.1)[69]. This fund also covers Northern Ireland, with DENI a co-funder of the proposals. It is envisaged that this will become a permanent new third stream of funding for HEIs, complementing existing streams for teaching and research. Focus is on improving the organisational arrangements and infrastructures in HEIs so that they can respond to business needs and develop greater access and use by business of HEIs. A desired emphasis is on building interactions with small companies (HEFCE, 1999, p.6). The fund proposes a maximum level of funding per HEI of £1.1m over four years with a total fund of £10m in 1999-2000 and £20m per annum thereafter. This and additional initiatives will be important to integrate mission and diffusion-oriented university research fully into the regional R&D system and strategy in Northern Ireland.

Grants and Assistance to R&D

7.8   Government grants and subsidies for private sector R&D in Northern Ireland are channelled primarily through IRTU[70]. IRTU, when established, took over many of the responsibilities of the former Technology Board for Northern Ireland (TBNI) and the R&D programme of IDB and the Local Enterprise Development Unit (LEDU)[71]. IRTU administers EU and international grants and subsidies for R&D that are

---

[69] *Business in the context of the proposals is defined to include Government research establishments and agencies.*

[70] *LEDU non-growth SMEs receive some funding directly from LEDU.*

[71] *For a description of Northern Ireland R&D policy prior to 1992, see NIEC (1993), Chapter 9.*

available to Northern Ireland businesses and universities, assisting them to access EU framework R&D funding through the EU Innovation Relay Centre that it operates jointly with LEDU. It acts as managerial agent for EU Objective 1 Structural and Special Programmes (eg the Technology Development Programme (TDP) and the IFI S&T Programme) and promotes the EU Fifth Framework Programme for R&D. It also facilitates Northern Ireland business and university participation in DTI initiatives, provides funds to the Northern Ireland Technology Centre (NITC) established at QUB in 1987, and implements the programme of Northern Ireland-United States co-operation announced at the White House Conference in 1995.

7.9   Table 7.2 gives a breakdown of the R&D expenditure administered by IRTU, 1992-98. The annual average expenditure of funds over these years was approximately £18m, of which £12m was Northern Ireland voted expenditure and £6m was EU and IFI funds. Of the voted expenditure an annual average of £1.2m went to universities and £11.3m to industry. Table 7.3 gives a breakdown of expenditure administered in 1996-97.

7.10   At the pre-competitive research end of R&D, START is the primary IRTU programme, with an average annual expenditure of almost £4m. START, known as the Science and Technology Programme (STP) before 1995, provides up to 50 per cent of eligible costs of strategic applied and industrially relevant research projects in companies and universities that are consistent with Foresight[72]. Support for any one project now has an upper limit of £2m, but Table 7.4 shows that the average offer, 1992-98, to 61 projects, was just over £0.5m. 40 companies (and the two universities) were awarded the 61 projects, out of 1,150 companies in Northern Ireland that are eligible to apply for

---

[72]   *In exceptional circumstances, industrially relevant strategic research undertaken within a university may be eligible for up to 100 per cent funding.*

TABLE 7.2

Expenditure Administered by IRTU, by Programmes, 1992-98, Current £

	1992 -95 £m	1995 -98 £m	Annual Average £m	To Universities £m	To Business £m
STP/START	12.4	10.2	3.7	1.2	2.5
PPD/COMPETE	19.6	20.0	6.7	-	6.7
Advertising & Publicity	1.3	1.1	0.4	-	0.4
Other	4.7	6.0	1.7	-	1.7
Total Voted	**38.0**	**37.3**	**12.5**	**1.2**	**11.3**
EU	12.2	13.7	4.3	2.6	1.7
IFI	4.5	2.7	1.2	1.1	0.1
Total Overall	**54.7**	**53.7**	**18.0**	**4.9**	**13.1**

TABLE 7.3

Expenditure Administered by IRTU, by Programmes, 1996-97, Current £

	To Universities £m	To Business £m	Total £m
START	1.5	2.0	3.5
COMPETE	0.9	6.1	7.0
Advertising & Promotion	-	0.4	0.4
Other	-	2.3	2.3
Total	**2.4**	**10.8**	**13.2**
EU	3.1	1.8	4.9
IFI	0.9	0.1	1.0
Total Overall	**6.4**	**12.7**	**19.1**

Note (for both Tables): University figures include joint university and business grants.

Source (for both Tables): IRTU

TABLE 7.4

IRTU Offers of Assistance, by Selected Programme, 1992-98

	1992-95 Number	1995-98 Number	Annual Average Number	Average Value £
STP/START	32	29	10	£536,000
PPD/COMPETE	473	557	172	£44,000
Total	505	586	182	-

Source: IRTU

funding[73]. For example, IRTU and Seagate Technologies contributed 50 per cent each to a £1.2m project in QUB and UU, including funding graduate and undergraduate courses in areas of interest to Seagate. Shorts Missiles, Northern Ireland Electricity and O'Kane Poultry also have important research links with the universities under this and other programmes[74].

7.11   At the near-market development end of R&D, COMPETE is the primary IRTU programme, part EU funded, with an average annual expenditure of almost £7m. COMPETE, known as the Product and Process Development Programme (PPD) before 1994, provides up to 40 per cent of eligible costs to market-led product and process development

---

73 *In practice, however, the client base is the large companies, given the type of projects that are funded. In 1996, the top 10 companies undertaking R&D in Northern Ireland accounted for 62 per cent of all R&D undertaken by industry (DED, 1997).*

74 *IRTU estimates that only 40 companies in Northern Ireland are involved in pre-competitive applied R&D, and all are IRTU clients. IRTU has a target of 25 new START projects involving enhanced R&D capabilities, 1998-2001.*

in companies. Support for any one project has an upper limit of £250,000, but Table 7.4 shows that the average offer, 1992-98, to 1,030 projects, was just over £44,000[75]. 442 companies were awarded the 1,030 projects, out of 1,150 companies in Northern Ireland that were eligible to apply for funding. The client base has risen from 151 companies in 1994 to the current 442 and the long-term IRTU goal is to have all eligible companies (all IDB clients and LEDU Growth companies) participate in the programme.

7.12   Other IRTU programmes include the Innovation Audit and Environmental Audit schemes, which cover up to 66 per cent of consultancy costs for companies, and the Design Directorate, which provides consultancy help to companies in design matters. In September 1997 the Innovation Credit Scheme was launched and funded by IRTU, with the involvement of LEDU and Local Enterprise Centres. This provides subsidised consultancy in new product and process development to SMEs at the NITC at QUB, or at UU.

7.13   National initiatives led by DTI and implemented in Northern Ireland by IRTU include the Teaching Company Scheme (TCS). This enables businesses to access expertise in the knowledge base through the involvement of graduates. Each TCS programme involves recruiting a graduate to build continuing capability into a company. Assistance of up to 60 per cent is available towards individual programme costs. Northern Ireland's participation in TCS is proportionately higher than other UK regions due to financial sponsorship from IRTU and the co-operation of QUB and UU[76]. The College Business Partnership scheme is a similar

---

[75] *Phase 1 grants, for project proposals, are funded at 50 per cent of eligible costs up to a maximum of £15,000 and Phase 2 grants, for the actual projects themselves, are funded up to 40 per cent of eligible costs up to a maximum of £250,000 (10 per cent additional if the project has strong environmental benefits, a provision withdrawn in July 1999).*

[76] *QUB and UU are ranked in the first three universities in the UK in terms of numbers*

scheme operated by IRTU and involves business and the colleges of further education. The SMART Awards are another DTI initiative that makes up to 10 awards and grants per year of up to nearly £143,000 each to individuals and small firms to develop innovative ideas. SMART is promoted locally by IRTU. LINK is another DTI initiative which covers 50 per cent of the costs of co-operative pre-competitive research between companies and universities in Northern Ireland and other regions of the UK.

7.14   The main EU Structural Fund programme co-ordinated by IRTU is the Technology Development Programme, which has been instrumental in recent years in building up applied research capability in Northern Ireland companies and universities. This is a pre-competitive programme which provides support for self-sustaining research infrastructure to assist in improving the competitiveness of Northern Ireland industry. STAR and STRIDE have been other special EU initiatives. Research centres of excellence in the universities, established under TDP, STAR and STRIDE, now number over 25 in Northern Ireland. These include the Northern Ireland Semiconductor Research Centre, the Queen's University Environmental Science and Technology Research Centre (QUESTOR), the Polymer Processing Research Centre, the Northern Ireland Bioengineering Centre (NIBEC), the Northern Ireland Centre for Diet and Health (NICHE), the Northern Ireland Knowledge Engineering Laboratory (NIKEL), the Engineering Composites Research Centre, the Northern Ireland Centre for Energy Research and Technology (NICERT) and the Northern Ireland Centre for Advanced Materials (NICAM). Examples of the size of some of the grants have been £2.7m to QUESTOR at QUB and £2.2m to NICAM, which is operated jointly by both UU and QUB. BCO Technologies base their R&D capability within the QUB Department of Electrical and Electronic Engineering under these programmes. Other European programmes include EUREKA, funding

of currently operating TCS programmes. The Northern Ireland Teaching Company Centre is by far the largest in the UK.

market-driven research projects by consortiums of European partners, ESPRIT, on information technology, and SPRINT, the Strategic Programme for Innovation and Technology Transfer.

7.15   Under its Science and Technology Programme, IFI has provided support to establish Technology Innovation Centres (TICs) in Northern Ireland to meet the needs of industry and, in addition, has provided 50 per cent funding support to projects involving cross-border co-operation and industry-university links.   In 1996 IFI introduced the Radius (now Radian) programme to support the establishment of joint ventures between Irish and North American companies for the purposes of new product and process development.   Examples of IFI funded centres include the Institute for Advanced Microelectronics, the Centre for Computing in Ireland, the Custom Chemical Synthesis Centre, the Product and Process Development Research Centre and the Joint Ceramics Research Centre and Surface Science Laboratory.

7.16   The Northern Ireland Innovation Programme (NIIP) is funded by LEDU and IFI as part of the EU's Business and Innovation Centre Programme.   It operates from regional innovation centres to give research and technical advice through universities and colleges.   The Technical Enterprise Programme (TEP) is a cross-border initiative funded by the Republic of Ireland's Industrial Development Authority (IDA) and LEDU to provide technical advice and business training to companies.   A partnership established in 1997 to identify, adapt and develop appropriate new technology for SMEs, Manufacturing Technology Partnership Ltd (MTP), is a partnership between DANI (Loughry College), QUB, UU and IRTU.   It is the result of dialogue between IRTU and the US Department of Commerce, and a decision to implement in Northern Ireland a programme modelled on a manufacturing extension programme piloted with considerable success in the US and designed to allow access for SMEs to university research facilities and expertise.

Intramural Department Expenditure

7.17   As Figure 7A shows, Northern Ireland Departments' expenditure on R&D in 1996-97, with the exception of R&D and technology support through IRTU, was aimed primarily at supporting their services and policy requirements, and not the science base. This is also made clear by Figure 7B, which shows that expenditure was largely towards the development end of the R&D spectrum, with 37 per cent in specific applied research, 36 per cent in development, and only 5 per cent in basic research. When DED expenditure is excluded (which is not intramural

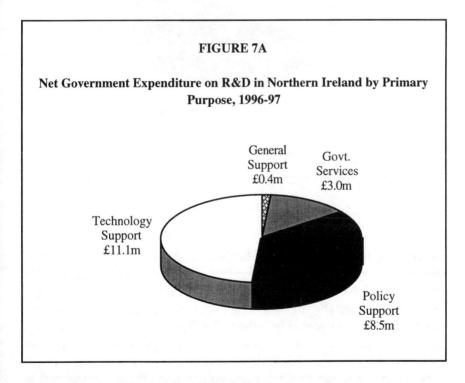

FIGURE 7A

Net Government Expenditure on R&D in Northern Ireland by Primary Purpose, 1996-97

General Support £0.4m

Govt. Services £3.0m

Technology Support £11.1m

Policy Support £8.5m

Source: DTI/ONS, 1998, p.20)

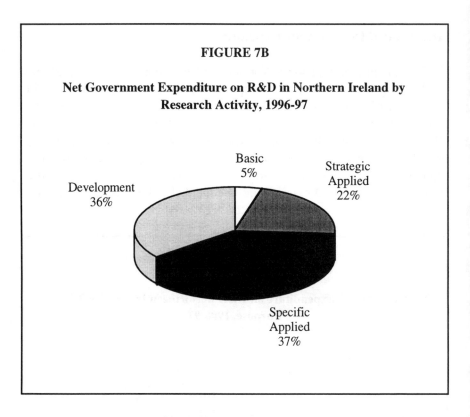

FIGURE 7B

Net Government Expenditure on R&D in Northern Ireland by Research Activity, 1996-97

Source: DTI/ONS (1998, p.23)

expenditure but R&D grants to business and university/business joint ventures through IRTU), DANI dominated intramural Government R&D expenditure in Northern Ireland in 1996-97 (Table 7.1), with 69 per cent of all expenditure (Figure 7C). This does not appear to be a strategic policy decision but probably reflects the Department's many statutory, operational and regulatory responsibilities and, perhaps, the historical patterns and priorities in Northern Ireland Government Department expenditure. Support of service and policy in the other Departments is much lower than in DANI.

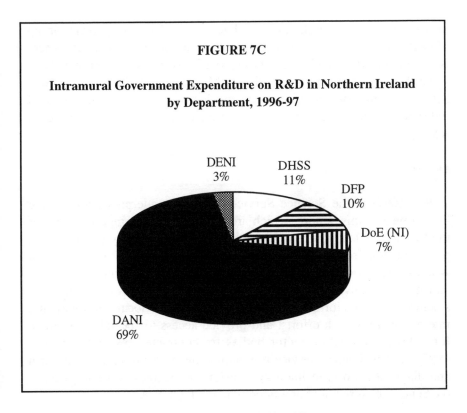

FIGURE 7C

Intramural Government Expenditure on R&D in Northern Ireland by Department, 1996-97

DENI 3%
DHSS 11%
DFP 10%
DoE (NI) 7%
DANI 69%

Source: DTI/ONS (1998, p.20)

7.18   OST guidelines for the use of scientific advice in Government policy making highlight three areas where scientific advice can make critical contributions in Departments - identifying issues, building science into policy, and presenting policy (OST, 1997, 1998). In Northern Ireland, DHSS has a standing expert advisory committee (to help identify issues) and the Research and Development Office (RDO). In order to build science into policy, the IRTU Chief Executive, as the DED's chief scientist and engineer, sits on the DED Board, and chairs a Research Liaison Group and Research Funders Group in the Northern Ireland Civil

Service (NICS). Scientific policy advice to the Top Management Group of DANI is provided by the Department's Chief Scientific Officer. There is close interaction at all levels throughout DANI between policy makers, scientific managers and scientists. Moreover, DANI has an R&D Strategy Committee providing the mechanism for the farm and food industry and the wider community to provide advice on the Department's R&D policy.

DANI

7.19   R&D in the Science Service of DANI underpins many of the Department's aims, among which are improving the competitiveness of the Northern Ireland agriculture, food, fisheries and forestry sectors, being proactive and responsive to the needs of consumers for safe and wholesome food, protecting animal welfare, and conserving and enhancing the environment. DANI's R&D strategy aims to develop the science base in Northern Ireland, contribute to local, national and international research efforts, and provide access to specialist expertise for industry and public sector bodies for contracted research (Davies, 1997)[77]. The Science Service programme integrates research, analytical and diagnostic work, technology transfer and degree-level education in the School of Agriculture and Food Science at QUB[78].

7.20   Divisions of the Science Service exist in Corporate Services, Food Science, Applied Plant Science, Agricultural and Environmental Science, Agricultural and Food Economics, and Veterinary Science. For example, DANI spends an annual £0.9m on research related to animal

---

[77] *DANI hence acts in R&D in a much different manner to the other Departments. Other Departments' expenditures are to support services and policy only, and not also to develop the science base. Again, the DANI/QUB link is relevant here.*

[78] *DANI believes there is a synergy between diagnostic and testing work, which accounts for about 50 per cent of activity of the science service, and R&D, which accounts for 30 per cent. Specialist advice and tertiary education accounts for the remaining 20 per cent.*

health and welfare, and £0.6m on research related to food safety (OST, 1999, p.32). The Agricultural Research Institute of Northern Ireland comes within the management of the Agricultural and Environmental Science Division. The DANI R&D Strategy Committee formed in 1996 with terms of reference to advise DANI on the research program and R&D strategy has members representing the interests of the Department, the farming and food industries (eg Moy Park, Leckpatrick Dairies and Northern Foods), farmers, environmental groups and consumers (eg a public health consultant). DANI also has formal R&D links with DoE (NI) via the DANI/DoE Scientific Liaison Committee, and with DHSS, via the Northern Ireland Food Surveillance Working Group. DANI is also represented on the UK Agriculture, Horticulture and Forestry Foresight Panel.

7.21 A distinctive institutional arrangement is that under the 1928 Queen's University Act, the School of Agriculture and Food Science is funded largely by DANI which guides and directs much of the research in the School. Academic staff at the QUB department hold joint appointments with DANI and are paid by DANI, which also funds around two-thirds of the costs of the School, the remaining one-third being derived from student fee income provided to the university by local authorities. This is not a unique arrangement (as noted in Section 6 above, in Scotland, The Netherlands, Denmark and Sweden agricultural universities and colleges are funded by Government Ministries), but it is a remarkable one. This QUB/DANI link provides a distinctive Northern Ireland model of Government-university R&D co-operation and collaboration, and ensures close interaction between the R&D needs of Government and industry and the pursuit of academic excellence[79].

---

[79] *A key recommendation of a Government review of public sector research establishments in the UK is that they should "develop effective formal links with universities where they do not exist at present" (Cabinet Office Efficiency Unit, 1994, p.17), cited by DANI (1998). The 1996 Research Assessment Exercise (RAE) gave QUB Agriculture a 5 ranking (UK average of 3.5) and QUB Food Sciences a 4 ranking (UK average of 2.7).*

DANI argues that the DANI/QUB link is regarded favourably within Northern Ireland and internationally and minimises the duplication of research efforts between DANI and QUB. Moreover, DANI funded research is not only subject to RAE but also DANI formal research review as to its relevance to the agri-food sector.

7.22   A significant interface exists between DANI and IRTU on sponsorship of R&D for the agri-food sector in Northern Ireland. DANI estimates that in 1995-96 IRTU funded £3.1m of R&D in the sector, £1.5m via the EU TDP, where DANI sits on the TDP selection committee, £1.3m via COMPETE, where food industry R&D projects are often subcontracted to DANI at Loughry College and QUB, and the remainder via START, mostly to QUB Food Science, where DANI sits on the IRTU Food Directorate which assesses applications for assistance under the START food programme. DANI also sits on the overall DED Food Liaison Group, where a DANI paper on R&D is to form part of a strategy document for the Northern Ireland food industry[80]. At the UK level, the Agriculture, Food and Fisheries Research Funders Group on which DANI is represented operates to keep under review requirements for publicly funded R&D and the requirements of industry and other users. Its first report (June 1997) showed no significant gaps or overlaps in funding at the UK level.

7.23   DANI also has research income of about £2.7m per annum from external research contracts undertaken for others. Most of the £2.7m is facilitated via The Queen's University Research Office and it is QUB rather than DANI that enters into contracts with commercial customers wishing to contract research through the School of Agriculture and Food Science. While it is DANI employees who manage and supervise such contracted research, the income from customers is managed through QUB accounts. The system provides another example of the DANI/QUB link in that, given the paucity of private sector resources in Northern Ireland

---

[80]   *All information supplied by DANI.*

for research in the agri-food sector, DANI, via the DANI/QUB link, can offer a research facility for those customers willing to pay, hence strengthening the interaction between public and private sector research in the agri-food area. DANI only undertakes contracted research on behalf of external, paying customers whose concerns align closely with DANI's departmental Aims and Objectives. About 40 per cent of receipts are from EU public bodies, 45 per cent from non-EU public bodies, and 15 per cent from private commercial bodies.

DoE (NI)

7.24   The Department of the Environment's R&D activity is largely statutory and regulatory based to enable it to carry out its responsibilities and strategic objectives. Expenditure amounts to over £1m largely in the Water Service, the Planning Service, the Environmental and Heritage Service (EHS), the Roads Service and the Northern Ireland Housing Executive. The EHS collaborates with Scottish authorities in the Scotland and Northern Ireland Forum for Environmental Research (SNIFFER), involving a shared research budget. It is also a partner in QUESTOR at QUB. Much work is survey-related such as the Northern Ireland Countryside Survey of the Natural Heritage Division of EHS. Other work is commissioned as part of major initiatives such as the Planning Service's Regional Strategy Framework for Northern Ireland (DoE (NI), 1998) and the Roads Service's Northern Ireland Strategic Transportation Model. The Water Service collaborates with their UK counterparts through United Kingdom Water Industry Research (UKWIR). Much of the research is contracted locally, since it depends on detailed localised knowledge of Northern Ireland.

DFP

7.25   The R&D budget of DFP of approximately £1m is expended on economic and social research primarily through the Northern Ireland Statistical and Research Agency (NISRA) and the DFP Economics

Division. NISRA provides a statistical and social research service to Northern Ireland departments and agencies, and supports the formulation, monitoring and evaluation of social policies. It is the Government's principal advisory body on statistics and social research. Although much of its activity is in statistical collection, publication and surveys, another portion can be classified as R&D. NISRA staff are stationed at agency headquarters in 9 internal branches and throughout the Northern Ireland Civil Service at 19 outposts, including the DED Statistics and Research Branch, the DANI Farm Survey Branch, DENI, the Central Statistics and Research Branch of DoE (NI), DHSS, Northern Ireland Office (NIO) and the Royal Ulster Constabulary (RUC). DFP Economics Division carries out and commissions research on local economic problems.

7.26   A major focus is the Central Community Research Unit (CCRU) whose research budget is managed by NISRA and whose Research Management Group is chaired by NISRA. The CCRU was established in 1987 and has published research strategies in 1991, 1995 and 1999. It encourages and supports academic teaching and independent research on the theory and practice of community relations and the evaluation of programmes. It has funded a considerable number of research projects, expending about £0.6m in 1996-97. NISRA also commissions research, largely from within Northern Ireland. Expenditure in 1997-98 was £507,000; £335,000 to Northern Ireland higher educational institutions, £145,000 to the Northern Ireland private sector, and £27,000 to universities external to Northern Ireland.

Other

7.27   Other agencies and publicly funded bodies might be considered to be associated with R&D in Northern Ireland. The Northern Ireland Economic Research Centre (NIERC) and NIEC do research on Northern Ireland economic issues, and DFP manages the various efficiency plans of the NICS/NIO - the Continuous Improvement Programme (CIP), the Business Development Service (BDS), the Northern Ireland Audit Office

(NIAO), and the Government Purchasing Agency (GPA). All of these are concerned with business process re-engineering and education in the public service, and innovation on current practices. For example, BDS provides business support services in telecommunications, management, training, IT and systems services, and other central business facilities to the public sector. There is also the Ordnance Survey (DoE (NI)), and the Forensic Science Agency of NIO might be considered to do some R&D in its support of law, order, protective and miscellaneous services in Northern Ireland.

The Health R&D Programme

7.28   An aim of the DHSS, as elucidated in the recently published document *Research for Health and Wellbeing: A Strategy for R&D to Lead Northern Ireland into the 21st Century* (HPSS, 1999) is that its service should be evidence-based and research-led. Until 1998-99, expenditure on R&D within the HPSS was supported by a range of mechanisms, including a departmental intramural R&D budget of about £1m (in the Information and Research Policy Branch), R&D expenditure by Boards and Special Agencies (largely in hospitals through the Health Trusts, and largely in turn in the Belfast City Hospital and the Royal Victoria Hospital), and a notional 25 per cent of Supplement for Teaching and Research funding to the hospitals. The latter amounted to about £6m but was not explicitly linked to actual R&D activity. Boards, Trusts and Agencies declared their non-commercial R&D activities, costs and related income for 1996-97 as part of the wide-ranging review of how R&D was conducted and funded within the National Health Service (the Culyer Report) and the declarations revealed spending of £12.8m as the net cost of R&D in the health service, compared with a notionally-funded level of £7.4m. This implied that £5.4m allocated for patient and client care was being diverted from these budgets and was being deployed instead on R&D. The declarations included research in personal social services as well as in health and primary care.

7.29   In April 1998 the HPSS R&D Office (RDO) was formally established as a directorate of the Central Services Agency, and at that time the HPSS R&D Fund was created[81]. The purpose was to establish and manage a single and transparent funding stream for all R&D in the HPSS for 1998-99 onwards and to develop a single, coherent and integrated R&D strategy for health and social care in Northern Ireland, acknowledging the special needs and problems of Northern Ireland. The R&D fund was established by DHSS at a much lower level than the estimated spending of £12m in 1996-97 and 1997-98, at £8.4m for 1998-99 and £9.4m for 1999-2000, to be used to deliver relevant and carefully targeted R&D. The role of the RDO is to manage the HPSS R&D Fund and to implement the HPSS R&D Strategy, which seeks to strategically co-ordinate R&D for the HPSS, and improve the methods used to identify, prioritise, manage and fund R&D. The Strategy's goal is to encourage a research literate HPSS, improve research staff capacity, and support an evidence-based and research-led HPSS. It is envisaged that in doing so, the profile of R&D will be raised, the relevance and quality of health R&D will improve and, in the face of finite resources, more focus, selectivity and coherence will be achieved.

7.30   The HPSS R&D Strategy was issued for directed consultation in April 1999 (HPSS, 1999). It argued that R&D effort in health in Northern Ireland has been fragmented in the past, and the lack of an HPSS R&D strategy has reduced the ability of the universities to become fully engaged with the research needs of HPSS. It highlights the need to harmonise the R&D strategy of HPSS with those of the universities, for example, through the formation of a Northern Ireland Forum for Health and Social Care Research[82]. The Strategy is now being operationalised through the publication of strategy papers for each of the nine strands of

---

[81]   *The RDO Director was appointed in 1997.*

[82]   *The possibility is also being explored of establishing a Northern Ireland Institution for Health and Social Care Research, linked to one or both of the universities. (HPSS, 1999, p.55)*

the Strategy[83].

7.31   Although the overall level of future R&D activity in the HPSS may be lower than in the recent past, it is felt that the HPSS R&D Strategy will increase its rigor, relevance, impact, accountability, transparency and co-ordination. One of the nine strands of activity involves Recognised Research Groups (RRGs). These multi-disciplinary research groups, once they are established and settled, will compete for funds, and will be encouraged also to win new external funding for health and social services (HSS) research in Northern Ireland. The RRG structure will ensure that this strand of the R&D fund is used to deliver high quality, relevant and co-ordinated programmes of R&D. Encouragement will be given to establishing a leading Northern Ireland role in focused areas of primary and community health and social care research.

7.32   Funding priorities will emerge from the nine strands of R&D activity and the specific research needs of the DHSS and HSS Boards will be met by the commissioned research strand. Needs for education and training will be met in another strand. It is hoped that the R&D strategy will increase the Northern Ireland share of health R&D investment in the UK, a share that has been low[84]. With respect to co-ordination with industry, the Northern Ireland Forum for Health and Social Care Research to be established will have representation from industry, NIGC, and IRTU through the Northern Ireland Life and Health Technologies Partnership. It is also proposed that a Northern Ireland Clinical Trials Centre be established. The circumscribed geographical and genetic characteristics of the Northern Ireland population provide an opportunity for Northern

---

83   *These nine strands range across such areas as education and training, commissioned research, career development, research groups and special initiatives.*

84   *There is little private industry support for health R&D in Northern Ireland due to a lack of companies in proximity. Since industry contracts tend to go to universities geographically close to the health and drug companies, collaboration with industry is limited in Northern Ireland since the companies are not here.*

Ireland to contribute to meeting the growing need for clinical trials.

The University R&D Programme

7.33   Other than in Agriculture and Food Science, DENI is the Government Department that in large part funds university R&D in Northern Ireland. It does this with the advice of the Northern Ireland Higher Education Council (NIHEC) whose recommendations are based mainly on the research funding model of the HEFCE. DENI institutional and infrastructural block funding is the major plank of the dual support system for university research in Northern Ireland, the other being special project-based funding from research councils (as in the rest of the UK). External income is generated from charities, Government and health authorities, industry, the EU and overseas, and other funding. Figure 7D below demonstrates that Northern Ireland universities depended in 1995-96 proportionally more on block, Government Department and health authority, and EU and overseas funding than universities in the rest of the UK, and proportionately less on industry, research council, and UK charities funding[85].

7.34   These differences can be explained in various ways. The low proportion of industry funding stems from the nature of the Northern Ireland industrial structure; the predominance of SMEs and of older, lower technology industries such as shipbuilding and textiles and clothing, the prevalence of external ownership, and the lack of companies, particularly pharmaceutical companies, headquartered in Northern Ireland[86]. The low proportion of research council and UK charities

---

[85]   *An analysis of sources of research income to QUB and UU in 1990-91 showed a similar pattern (NIEC, 1993, Table 8.2, p.127).*

[86]   *As fully documented in NIEC (1993). A recent NIERC survey indicates that only 2 per cent of non-university spin-out SMEs in Northern Ireland have research links with the universities. Economic structure in Northern Ireland limits business R&D activity in general and links to the universities in particular.*

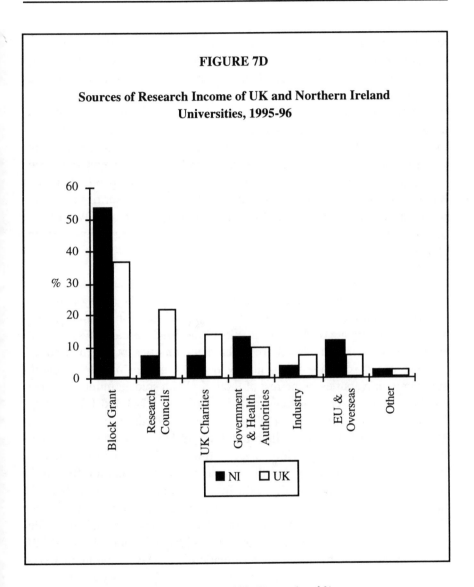

FIGURE 7D

Sources of Research Income of UK and Northern Ireland Universities, 1995-96

Source: Hughes (1998, Figures 1 and 2)

funding perhaps reflects relatively low RAE ratings in 1992 and the fact that university researchers in Northern Ireland tend to look to other funds for support. The high level of EU and overseas funding reflects Northern Ireland's success in generating EU funds due to its Objective 1 status in the 1990s and substantial experience in accessing EU funds, and status as a region for international support efforts such as IFI. The higher proportion of Government and health authority funding reflects, in general, the Northern Ireland Government's special needs for local research due to the wide range of devolved public responsibilities under unique circumstances, and, in particular, IRTU as a sponsor of university research, for example, via the Teaching Company Scheme (SQW, 1996), and the relatively advantageous access to Government grants in Northern Ireland.

7.35   From 1993-94 onwards, universities in Northern Ireland, as in the rest of the UK, ceased to receive research funding on the basis of student numbers. Funding became Quality Related and tied for each academic Unit of Assessment (UoA) to the results of the 1992 Research Assessment Exercise (RAE). The Northern Ireland universities research funding became based selectively on quality in the same manner as research funding to universities in the rest of the UK. With student number-related funding for research removed and with UoAs at QUB and UU scoring below UK averages in general in the 1992 RAE, Northern Ireland faced a £9m cut in block funding. Such a cut would have devastated the local research base, but the previous level of funding (£25m) was maintained with the introduction of Northern Ireland Developmental Research (NIDevR) funding of initially £9m for three years. Although NIHEC argued for the maintenance of university research funding at least at former levels (equivalent to the original £25m), the funding available from DENI was cut by £4m in 1997-98 and by a further £2m in 1998-99[87]. In the event this led to the termination of NIDevR funding in 1998-

---

[87]   *From 1997-98 on only UoAs achieving RAE grades of 3b or better received QR research funding. Some support was provided to the NIDevR initiative from EU Funds.*

99.

7.36   NIDevR funding was allocated on a competitive basis through the Research Sub-committee of NIHEC, which included among its membership representatives of the business and academic communities and members of relevant Government departments, such as DANI and IRTU. NIDevR was allotted on the principles of increasing research quality, ensuring greater contribution of research to the economic, social and cultural life of Northern Ireland, achieving greater success in relating research to the needs of industry, increasing the levels of research funding, and improving links with other universities, research establishments and industry. The results of NIDevR have been argued to have been positive (SQW, 1996; 1997). The funds were allocated on the basis of bids from the universities which included the requirement for them to develop and articulate coherent and cost-effective research strategies. Funds were closely monitored which made the universities more accountable and encouraged them to install new internal research monitoring and management procedures[88]. Most expenditure was on new academic staff which led to faculty renewal. Greater success in relating research to local needs was secured[89], but some conflict between doing research relevant to local industry and Government and doing research to achieve high RAE scores (the latter demanding research of a basic, internationally-recognised nature) was admitted (SQW, 1996).

7.37   Northern Ireland universities, in addition to QR block funding from DENI, receive Generic Research (GR) funding, introduced in response to the DTI Science and Technology White Paper, *Realising our Potential* (DTI, 1993). GR provides incentives to universities to conduct research collaboratively with users of research in industry and the

---

[88]   *The UU Research Office was established in 1993-94 and the QUB Research Management Unit in 1994-95.*

[89]   *For example, The Queen's Institute of Criminology and Criminal Justice was established at the specific request of the Northern Ireland Office.*

community at large, with a funding contribution from DTI. With NIDevR phased out from 1998-99, the balance of DENI funding (other than QR and GR) of about £3m has been allocated on the basis of RAE quality ratings and is conditional on each university producing an updated research strategy which included specific recognition of the economic, social and cultural needs of Northern Ireland and of collaboration with other organisations. HEFCE's strategy to ensure that higher education is responsive to the needs of industry is hence mirrored by DENI (OST, 1999, p.55).

7.38   With regard to collaboration with industry, both universities have a number of applied research centres designed specifically to serve the needs of Northern Ireland industry. These include, for example, NICAM, NIBEC, QUESTOR and NITC, all mentioned above. Government has done much during recent years to encourage a partnership approach by using EU funds to improve the university infrastructure for R&D, since the universities play a vital role in providing much of the R&D infrastructure in Northern Ireland (Beatty, 1997). In order to develop an infrastructure of R&D Centres, the universities have received in recent years investments approaching £30m from the EU Structural Funds and Special Initiatives, and have had access to IRTU START financing. Also, IFI has funded the development of collaborative multi-site R&D Centres on an all-Ireland basis. Through NICAM, Seagate Technologies, UU and QUB are involved in a joint £2m R&D Consortium, all made possible by IRTU and DENI NIDevR funding. Nortel Networks have also recently announced a major joint R&D consortium with the two universities (the Jigsaw Project) involving a £3m investment by Nortel and IRTU. The Digital Signal Processing (DSiP) Laboratories at QUB are another £1.2m investment.

7.39   The mission statement of QUB confirms a commitment to assist in the social and economic development of Northern Ireland:

The University is conscious of its regional responsibility as a major centre of knowledge, learning and scholarship and as a major provider of the research infrastructure of Northern Ireland. We will provide a broad research base which will facilitate applied research and knowledge transfer to satisfy the needs of business, industry, government and the wider community (Beatty, 1997).

QUB has established R&D and technology transfer centres which have a prime aim of providing direct and rapid assistance to local industry with particular focus on the needs of SMEs. In addition, in 1985, a venture capital company, QUBIS Ltd, was established to identify R&D projects which have the potential for commercial exploitation and to assist such projects through from incubation to the market place (Beatty, 1997). This is done by the formation of new subsidiary enterprises in which academic staff take shares in joint ventures with QUBIS Ltd or other established firms or both. The aim of QUBIS Ltd is to make profitable returns, to assist the transfer of university knowledge, and to assist economic development (Blair and Hitchins, 1998). To date 20 enterprises have been established, employing in excess of 350, mostly graduates, with a total turnover in excess of £15m. Examples include KAINOS Software and Andor Technology.

7.40   UU calculate their research activities at £25m per year involving 500 academic staff engaged in research rated in the RAE at 3a (national standard) and above, 200 contract research staff, and 700 research students (UU, 1998). The university has ten applied research centres supported by the EU and IFI, and these centres are its primary vehicles for technology transfer[90]. Another is UUTECH, the university's technology

---

[90]   *For example, the Northern Ireland Centre for Health Information, NIKEL (a joint venture with ICL), and others as noted above. A new centre of excellence in e-commerce is under proposal.*

transfer company, established in 1997. This is an umbrella company to take stake in spin-out and start-up companies, to negotiate intellectual property rights, to lease out incubator units, and to manage consultancy activities. With the support of DED, the university has established high technology incubator units at its campuses in Coleraine, in life and health technologies, and in Derry. The Technology and Software Incubator Centre at Magee College in Derry is a £2.7m investment.

7.41   Both QUB and UU have staff who co-ordinate industrial and commercial liaison and facilitate access to the most appropriate expertise. In recent years both universities have restructured the co-ordination of all aspects of research administration within specialist Research Offices. The universities have been closely involved in the work of the NIGC Technology Partnerships and the Northern Ireland Foresight Programme with university staff serving on the Foresight Steering Committee and on each of its six Sector Panels. The Research Offices of the universities are responsible for implementing research policy and ensuring quality of research. In 1993 both QUB and UU began programmes to develop their research in terms of quality and relevance to Northern Ireland under NIDevR, contributing significantly to the improved research grades achieved in the 1996 RAE (Beatty, 1997). QUB has also recently established a Regional Office to deal with liaison with public agencies and private companies.

Conclusion

7.42   Before going on to an assessment of the strategy of publicly funded R&D in Northern Ireland in Section 8, what can be said in conclusion to this section in answer to the question regarding the private and publicly funded R&D system in Northern Ireland posed at the beginning of the report; what is the nature of the system, and of co-ordination and co-operation between Government, universities and industry (question 5, p.4)?

7.43   It is apparent from the descriptive summary of this section that there is in Northern Ireland quite an impressive array of R&D capabilities in the publicly funded and private R&D spend, and some important co-ordination and collaboration initiatives.   Foresight, NIGC/IRTU Technology Partnerships, IRTU, EU and IFI funds to build up applied research capability in Northern Ireland companies and universities, the QUB/DANI link, NIDevR and GR, QUBIS and UUTECH have all increased the contribution of research to the economic, social and cultural life of Northern Ireland, achieved success in relating research to the needs of industry and improved links between Government, university and business research and innovation. New initiatives such as the Reach Out Fund, the Science Park, the University Challenge Fund and the NI R&D Challenge Fund promise more.

7.44   While there is much excellent work going on and in the pipeline, it cannot be said that the overall system constitutes a co-ordinated and co-operative regional R&D community. Beyond the Foresight exercise, specific inter-departmental (eg DANI/IRTU/DED and DANI/DoE (NI)) initiatives, and the academic-industry links fostered by IRTU and the DANI/QUB link, there appears to be no formal overall knowledge management co-ordination. There is no overall Inter-Department Committee on R&D, no overall R&D budget, and IRTU does not appear to have the means and policy levers at its disposal to fully manage and co-ordinate the publicly funded R&D spend across Government Departments, the health sector, the universities and industry.

7.45   In 1993 the Council made recommendations regarding the R&D system in Northern Ireland (NIEC, 1993). Given that Northern Ireland lacks the R&D infrastructure of national industrial research association, research council and Government laboratories that exists in most other regions of the UK, and that private sector R&D is relatively low, the Council encouraged IRTU and the universities to take the leading roles in the R&D system. It recommended that the universities develop long-term strategies for R&D, formulated and implemented in consultation with

DED through IRTU, and that the latter, whose chief executive serves the role of Government chief engineer and scientist, should oversee and co-ordinate private, Government and university R&D. For example, the Council stated that it was its view that "... it is not possible for IRTU to maximise progress towards its aim[s] ... if it does not have an input at least on an advisory basis into the development of R&D strategy within the two local universities" (p.145).

7.46   This vision for the Northern Ireland publicly funded R&D system has not been wholly realised, and the system remains largely uncoordinated between IRTU, the other Government Departments, the universities and industry. IRTU influence extends only to its programme of grant-assisted industrial R&D projects and funding of university capabilities and academic-industry links through EU and IFI funds. Initiatives to commercialise the results of R&D in the universities, health authorities and Government Departments appear to be largely left to the institutions themselves, with no overall programme. Beyond the publicly funded NIGC initiative, Government appears to have taken a largely hands-off approach to linkages and networking, while at the same time individual R&D activities are supplemented by a hands-on approach of grants and subsidies.

7.47   How might the Northern Ireland system be categorised, in light of the alternative systems of R&D in the other nations and regions discussed in Section 6 above? Fundamentally, Northern Ireland seems to have a diffuse and grant-driven system of R&D, not a concentrated and co-ordinated policy-led system. This encourages grant-seeking, but not linkages, networking and co-ordination and not a consensual strategy for R&D and innovation. The development of a Northern Ireland Science Park might help to re-define the system (as long as it is not just tacked onto it) but it is clear that much more needs to be done before the different programmes in Northern Ireland are broken out of their current silos and fully integrated and co-ordinated.

7.48   It cannot be said that Northern Ireland has either a cluster-based system (Scotland), a sector-led system (Yorkshire and Humberside), any hybrid in between (Wales), or a foreign investment plus linkages system (formerly in Wales and the RoI). There are of course some aspects of cluster or sectoral strategy (NIGC) but this has been largely based on bench-marking and supply chain development rather than on R&D and S&T. The university-industry links approach characteristics of many jurisdictions (UK, North East England, Wales, Scotland) does also appear in Northern Ireland through the IRTU programme but such links in Northern Ireland are largely based on individual firm and university initiatives rather than on an overall strategy.   Neither is there a co-ordinated focus on R&D diffusion into innovation around a Knowledge House or Bridge concept, as found in other regions (South Sweden, Wales, North East England). Moreover, the embedding of the R&D and innovation system within a knowledge-driven economic development strategy with balanced and strategic attention to business, Government and university R&D, both mission and diffusion oriented, and with collaboration and co-operation between public and private institutions, which comes across in the models of R&D policy followed in many jurisdictions (UK, Denmark, The Netherlands and Wales) does not come across in an examination of the system in Northern Ireland.   Nor has Northern Ireland initiated the development of a RIS within which to place the public and private R&D system, as has been done in other comparable regions, and based on various alternative models.

7.49   Imbalance in the Northern Ireland system lies in the dominance of public-sector R&D capabilities in Government (especially DANI and the universities) and the lack of research institutions outside Government and the universities. Focus of R&D strategy has therefore been quite rightly on building up private sector capabilities relative to public through encouragement of R&D in indigenous companies and R&D-intensive foreign direct investment and on channelling university R&D to commercial exploitation through university spin-outs.   However, industry-academic links are not co-ordinated at regional Government level and appear to be largely driven by individual firm and university initiatives and by grant-seeking through IRTU, EU and IFI funds. The system is somewhat ad hoc. It cannot be characterised as either a sector or cluster-based system, or as a co-ordinated and balanced public-private partnership directed by a dedicated unit of Government, channelled through a regional R&D and innovation strategy, and mainstreamed into economic development and competitiveness strategy.

8 ASSESSMENT OF PUBLICLY FUNDED R&D STRATEGY IN NORTHERN IRELAND

Introduction

8.1   In this section the publicly funded R&D strategy in Northern Ireland is assessed in regard to the major themes and programmes identified in Section 7 - overall co-ordination, networking and linkages, R&D grants and assistance, intramural Department expenditure, the health R&D programme and the university R&D programme - before concluding with an overall assessment of R&D strategy and policy. In assessing the strategy close attention is paid to the questions posed in the introduction to the report (para 1.5). Answers to questions 1 to 5 have been provided in the previous Sections 4 to 7. Answers to questions 8 to 10 are attempted in Section 9 with recommendations for policy. This section then attempts to answer questions 6 and 7:

- Does there exist any unexploited potential for co-ordination and synergy in public funding of R&D in Northern Ireland, or gaps where additional investment would be beneficial, and is there an adequate level of co-ordination of R&D spending and programme delivery between Government, industry and the universities?

- is Northern Ireland achieving maximum economic benefit from its public R&D spend?

8.2   In attempting to answer these questions, this section will, *inter alia*, deal with questions such as whether the correct balance of publicly versus privately funded R&D is being struck in Northern Ireland strategy; whether the current allocation of activity across Government Departments is correct and sufficiently flexible to be revised according to changing needs and circumstances; whether the strategy is providing the correct incentives for public and private R&D, especially for R&D in SMEs, for the commercialisation of publicly funded R&D in universities, hospitals and Government departments, and for encouraging and maintaining high quality in R&D; and whether spillovers between R&D programmes, between public and private R&D, and between R&D in Northern Ireland and abroad, are being adequately encouraged and captured by the strategy.

Overall Co-ordination, Networking and Linkages

8.3   The major programmes in Northern Ireland appear to be largely in isolation to each other, with inadequate co-ordination both within each programme and between programmes, and imbalanced attention to public and private R&D in overall strategy. For example, within the intramural Department programme, there appears to be no clear rationale as to why DANI expenditure dominates and as to why expenditure within DoE (NI) is so much lower. The IRTU programme of grants to business does not appear to be systematically linked to the R&D capabilities in the public sector, and the capabilities of the two universities are not systematically co-ordinated. The health programme appears to sit in isolation and does not appear to be effectively linked to commercialisation or to the university programme. The same indeed might be said of the departmental intramural programme, with the possible exception of DANI/QUB R&D in the agri-food sector. The Northern Ireland Foresight exercise does not appear to have resulted in significant refocusing and concentration on key initiatives and their co-ordination within the overall publicly funded and private R&D programme, although the development of the Science Park might help do this. For example, a number of Government departments and agencies, and the two universities, have e-commerce initiatives, and there is seemingly overlap, duplication and diffusion of effort, with inadequate co-ordination and co-operation.

8.4   The incomplete accounting, monitoring, reporting of all public and private R&D expenditure in Northern Ireland by IRTU/DED, noted in Section 4 above, is symptomatic of this lack of co-ordinated attention in Government to both public and private R&D capabilities. The recently published draft economic development strategy, *Strategy 2010*, does better in more accurately reporting total R&D in Northern Ireland as summing to about 1.0 per cent of GDP (Economic Development Strategy Review Steering Group, 1999, p.117) but goes on to target only business expenditure for increase, and not total public and private expenditure (p.221), again symptomatic of a lack of co-ordinated attention to total R&D capabilities.

8.5   However, one example of where the philosophy of co-ordination and networking and concentration of emphasis is occurring in Northern Ireland is the Technology Partnerships promoted by NIGC. These are attempts to create networks at the sectoral level, with leadership being taken by the private sector through NIGC, but in co-operation with public sector players. The NIGC and the universities are creating, through the Partnerships, forums for networking, education and co-ordination to encourage technology transfer and innovation. More such actions and deliberations at the sectoral level are required, including the participation of more actors, such as IRTU, DoE (NI) and HPSS. In a recent study for the Economic Council, Dunford and Hudson (1996) welcomed the emphasis of the NIGC on assisting networks of firms, working and co-operating together, rather than individual firms, but they noted that there remains a need in Northern Ireland to develop a more systematic and integrated approach to R&D and innovation between the public and private sectors and a need to capitalise on links outside the region.

8.6   Another initiative in building capabilities is the Business Excellence Programme run by IDB in close co-operation with the Northern Ireland Quality Centre, which aims to encourage best practice in local companies through self-assessment and bench-marking techniques. There is also the International Partnership Programme, which helps local manufacturing and tradeable service companies enhance their ability to develop new international business opportunities through strategic alliances and partnerships. Furthermore, IDB client executives work closely with the NIGC to increase what Storper (1995) has called "untraded interdependencies" between firms within particular sectors, increasing firms' abilities to organise resources at their disposal to exploit productive opportunities. Such linkages can be an important conduit for new knowledge and economic development. More initiatives along these lines would be useful, modelled perhaps on the Welsh Technology Clubs or Forums, the NIGC Technology Partnerships and the CBI national strategy for bench-marking, "Fit for the Future".

8.7   On the other hand, an obvious area where co-operation and collaboration between Government, business and universities in Northern Ireland falls short is in the area of developing a Regional R&D and Innovation Strategy. The Competitiveness White Paper gives the new English RDAs the task of preparing regional innovation strategies to provide improved frameworks for innovation in their regions, as well as the task of developing, promoting and implementing their own strategies for improving regional economic performance and enhancing regional competitiveness. A regional innovation strategy, developed in concert between Government, industry and the universities, can form a core and focus for the overall R&D and economic development strategy of a region. Strong regional networks and other partnerships are required to be forged from a regional innovation strategy in order to develop a strategic long-term vision and plan for promoting regional economic competitiveness.

Bench-marking R&D Priorities

8.8   A way to view the question of overall co-ordination into a regional R&D strategy is to bench-mark Northern Ireland practice against best practice in R&D policy in other regions, such as those examined in Section 6 above. Table 8.1 lists the institutions and policy initiatives identified in Section 6 in these other regions for the co-ordination of private and publicly funded R&D and checks for their presence in Northern Ireland. Northern Ireland has at present only 3 of the 17 initiatives listed, and of these, only the two based on Foresight involves all the main players in the system - Government, universities, other public institutions, and industry. The Economic Development Strategy Review

TABLE 8.1

Bench-marking Northern Ireland Against Best Practice in R&D Policy

	Institution/Policy Initiative	Presence in NI
1	Minister for Research, S&T or IT	No
2	Office or Directorate for S&T	No
3	Foresight	Yes
4	Inter-Departmental S&T Committee	No
5	Ministerial/Cabinet S&T Committee	No
6	Advisory Council for S&T	No
7	RTP, RIS/RITTS	No
8	R&D Targets	No
9	Science Budget	No
10	Single Programme for R&D	No
11	Overall R&D Strategy	No
12	Commercialisation Initiatives	Yes[1]
13	RDA, Economic Development Agency	No
14	Sector-Based Technology Forums	Yes[2]
15	Embedding R&D Strategy Into Economic Development Strategy	No
16	Knowledge Bridge or House	No
17	(Limited Term) Contractual R&D Arrangements	No

[1] *University-led (QUBIS and UUTECH)*

[2] *Through NIGC and Foresight*

Source: Section 6 above

Steering Group (1999) *Strategy 2010*, does recommend new initiatives such as an Information Age Commission, and a business-sector R&D target, which partially mirror two of the initiatives in Table 8.2 (the

TABLE 8.2

R&D Expenditure[1] of Northern Ireland Departments, 1997-98 to 2001-02, Actual, Estimated and Planned, £m, Constant £

	Actual	Estimated	Plan	Provisional Plans	
	1997-98	1998-99	1999-2000	2000-01	2001-02
DANI	7.7	7.5	7.3	7.4	7.2
DED	10.4	10.5	12.6	13.9	14.4
DENI	0.2	0.3	0.4	0.0	0.0
DoE (NI)	0.8	0.9	1.0	0.9	0.9
DFP	1.4	1.4	1.4	1.9	1.8
DHSS	2.1	9.0	8.1	8.4[2]	8.1[2]
Total	22.7	29.6	31.3	32.5	32.4
of which:					
Intramural	9.4	9.3	9.0	8.8[2]	8.6[2]
Non-DED	12.3	19.1	18.7	18.6	18.0

[1] *Figures relate to Department plus RDO expenditure in DHSS, except 1997-98 which relate to Department expenditure only, excluding RDO.*

[2] *Figures are not available and nominal expenditure is assumed to continue at the same level as in 1999-2000.*

Source: OST (1999, p.83), deflated by implicit price index used by OST for UK R&D expenditure

Directorate for S&T and the R&D target). But there is much more that could be done in Northern Ireland to co-ordinate the overall public R&D spend and exploit synergy between public and private spending. As already noted in Section 6 best practice in other regions includes:

• high policy priority given to R&D and innovation;

• centralised institutions to implement and monitor this policy priority;

• mechanisms and institutions to ensure that the public R&D spend is continuously revised in response to changing priorities; and,

• full embedding of R&D policy into innovation, economic development and competitiveness strategy.

How does Northern Ireland measure up to these themes with respect to R&D funding and policy priorities?

R&D Funding Priorities

8.9   As already noted in Section 4 above, there is a downward trend in real public funding of R&D in Northern Ireland, at least since 1993-94, in universities, departments, and other public institutions, in contrast to an upward trend in business expenditure, promoted and partially funded by Government. The downward trend is clear from *Forward Look 1999* (OST, 1999). As Table 8.2 and Figures 8A, 8B and 8C show, these trends are forecast to continue to be downward over the period 1999-2000 to 2001-02 for most sectors of the public R&D spend with the exception of grants through IRTU for business sector research, which are projected to rise. These forecast downward trends contrast quite sharply with forecast upward trends in many areas of public funding, especially in universities, in the rest of the UK.

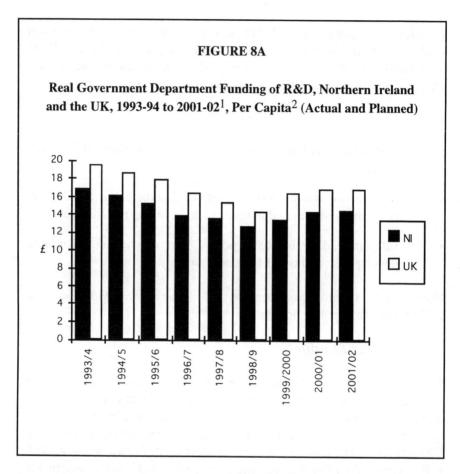

FIGURE 8A

Real Government Department Funding of R&D, Northern Ireland and the UK, 1993-94 to 2001-02[1], Per Capita[2] (Actual and Planned)

[1] *Figures exclude NHS/HPSS health R&D expenditures, but include DED/IRTU for Northern Ireland and OST/DTI for UK.*

[2] *Based on 1997 population for Northern Ireland of 1.675m and for UK of 59.009m (ONS, 1999, Table 1.2, p.30).*

Source: OST (1999, pp.66, 83). Expenditures are adjusted for inflation

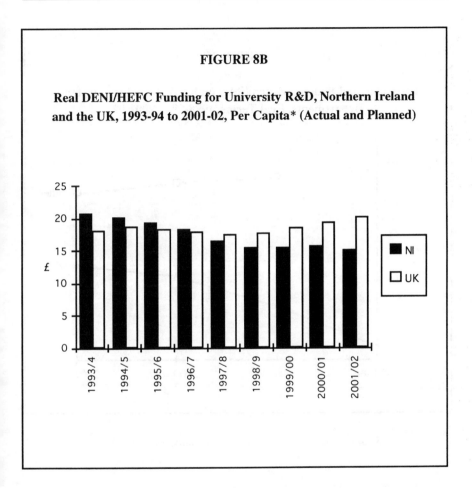

FIGURE 8B

Real DENI/HEFC Funding for University R&D, Northern Ireland and the UK, 1993-94 to 2001-02, Per Capita* (Actual and Planned)

* Based on 1997 population for Northern Ireland of 1.675m and for UK of 59.009m (ONS, 1999, Table 1.2, p.30).

Source: OST (1999, p.93) and DTI/ONS (1998, Table 5.3, p.44). Expenditures are adjusted for inflation

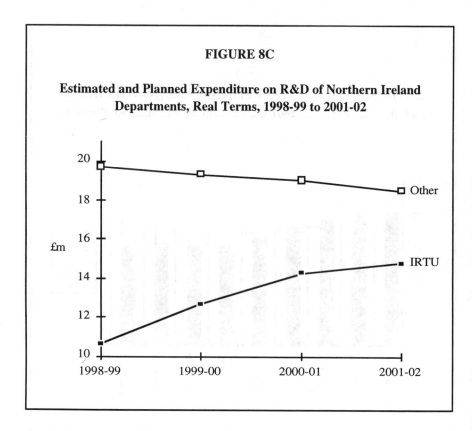

FIGURE 8C

Estimated and Planned Expenditure on R&D of Northern Ireland Departments, Real Terms, 1998-99 to 2001-02

Source: OST (1999, p.83). Figures are adjusted for inflation

R&D Policy Priorities

8.10   Soon after the publication by DED of *Innovation 2000* and the establishment of IRTU, both in 1992, the Council reported fully on R&D in Northern Ireland (NIEC, 1993). In its report the Council reiterated its belief that "the primary objective of economic policy should be to maximise growth in the economy (p.146)", and that "R&D is an important driving force behind economic growth" (p.8). The Council concluded,

> therefore, that policies aimed at improving the level of R&D in Northern Ireland and the rate at which the fruits of R&D are commercially exploited should form a central plank of an industrial development strategy which has the ultimate goal of generating economic growth and sustainable employment. This is not to overestimate the importance of R&D. Investment in physical capital and human resources is also vital (NIEC, 1993, p.147).

The report encouraged "IRTU, the universities and DENI to adopt a cohesive approach to R&D policy within Northern Ireland" (p.145), and recommended that university research be a key area of discussion for the Board of IRTU. Moreover, it stressed that R&D and innovation policy in Northern Ireland must form a central plank of the Government's overall industrial development strategy, with the ultimate goal of generating economic growth and sustainable employment (p.147).

8.11 Recent OECD recommendations regarding R&D and technology policy are summarised in Box 2 (OECD, 1998a). As OECD states with regard to these policies: "The key factor for success is the extent to which co-ordination can be achieved between ministries and relevant stakeholders who participate in the formation of policy" (OECD, 1998a, p.15). The OECD recommendations stress the need for co-operation, collaboration, co-ordination, and partnership between Government, industry, universities and other stakeholders in the making of R&D policies and the embedding of such policies within the broader policy agenda. As OECD states: "The purpose of R&D policy is to ensure that progress in knowledge translates into maximum social and economic benefits" (p.104).

BOX 2

Recent OECD Recommendations on R&D and Technology Policy

1. R&D and technology policies need to become an integral part of the broader policy agenda.

2. Policymakers must improve the management of the science base, increasing flexibility in research structures and increasing the incentives for university-industry collaboration. The correct balance between core and contact-based research has to be struck.

3. There is a need for greater involvement by industry, universities and other stakeholders in setting R&D priorities.

4. There must be adequate public financing of basic research.

5. The scope and design of financial support for industrial R&D must be assessed in order to increase transparency and efficiency.

6. Public-private partnerships in R&D should be encouraged and obstacles to international technological co-operation should be removed.

7. Improved inter-ministerial co-ordination, involving monitoring of implementing is required.

Source: OECD (1998a, p.15)

8.12   The recommendations of the recent UK Competitiveness White Paper (DTI, 1998) are broadly consistent with those of OECD: in fact OECD commends the UK (along with Denmark, Netherlands, Finland and the United States) as a nation where improvements along the lines they recommend are being implemented. The White Paper recognises that competitiveness is largely a private sector phenomenon but highlights three key points of leverage for Government in promoting competitiveness in the knowledge economy: strengthening capabilities; encouraging collaboration to compete; and encouraging competition. The White Paper recognises that Government has a role to play in competitiveness as a direct investor in the economy's knowledge base, but also as the creation of the environment in which business can invest in R&D.

8.13   In order to ensure that R&D translates into maximum social and economic benefits in Northern Ireland, the industrial, Government and university sectors must co-operate and collaborate if they are to proportionately match the research results of larger nations and regions. Limited R&D resources must be concentrated if Northern Ireland is to use R&D as a means of advancing economic growth and industrial competitiveness. Moreover, Northern Ireland players must forge international links, as emphasised also by OECD, to create the necessary scale and critical mass required in pre-competitive and basic research in order that it can further the cause of regional competitiveness.

8.14   Indicative of the fact that recommendations along the lines of those made by OECD and the Competitiveness White Paper are not currently being implemented in Northern Ireland is a comparison of the Comprehensive Spending Review in the UK with Northern Ireland (HM Treasury, 1998, and DFP/HM Treasury, 1998). As already noted in Section 6, the UK CSR gave prominent priority to S&T, R&D and the knowledge-based economy. However, the CSR in Northern Ireland makes little reference to these issues, despite the principal aim of Government: "To achieve peace, stability and *prosperity* in Northern

Ireland" [emphasis supplied], and "to achieve sustained economic growth and improved competitiveness in Northern Ireland's economy through education, employment and investment" (DFP/HM Treasury, 1998, p.5). High priorities are noted in law and order, health and education, but not in R&D and S&T[91].

8.15   *Strategy 2010* makes some recommendations regarding R&D policy in the economy. More resources are recommended for university-business collaboration, and the sectoral approach of NIGC in nurturing networks and improved sectoral competitiveness is fully endorsed, with the additional support of the social partners. Indeed, the strategy strongly endorses the principles of public-private partnership, collaboration and co-ordination in the development of the economy - presumably, also in the development of a Northern Ireland R&D strategy. One of *Strategy 2010's* 10 targets for the economy in 2010 is a level of business R&D as a percentage of GDP of 1.5 per cent, a level that currently sits at 0.6 per cent, but as noted above, there is no target set for overall R&D spend as a percentage of GDP, and no discussion of actual figures for increased public funding of R&D, although the inference is that such funding should be increased in order to complement such a large targeted increase in private sector spending.

8.16   A fundamental problem is that Northern Ireland's R&D and innovation strategy and system is not fully integrated into the Government's overall strategy for economic development. There is scope for some key players, notably the universities, to play a greater role in the regional R&D and innovation strategy. R&D, knowledge creation and innovation are not as high a public policy priority in economic development as they should be. There are weak and missing links in the network of relationships between Government, universities and industry and a lack of co-ordination, co-operation and collective effort in R&D initiatives. The result has been that Northern Ireland, despite its potential,

---

91   *The Science Centre portion of the Odyssey Project is, however, duly noted.*

has not been able to contribute a healthy share of UK, European and global investment in R&D, or contribute its proportionate share of innovation. The outcome is the continuing productivity gap between Northern Ireland and its economic neighbours.

Grants and Assistance for R&D

8.17   With regard to IRTU expenditure on R&D grants, which covers all the schemes mentioned above in Section 7, this in fact declined over the period 1992-93 to 1997-98. After starting at £27.5m in 1992-93, grant expenditure declined to £12.7m in 1996-97, before recovering to £17.7m in 1997-98[92]. Grants can be broken down into those to companies and those to universities, either solely or in partnership with a company. While assistance to companies changed little in real terms, 1992-93 to 1997-98, this expenditure however leveraged increasing levels of private sector R&D over these years. As noted in Table 8.2 and Figure 8C above, Northern Ireland voted expenditure on R&D grants through IRTU/DED is planned to increase over the next three years, consistent with recommendations in *Strategy 2010* that efforts to increase R&D in indigenous firms in Northern Ireland should be intensified.

8.18   Analysis of IRTU grants shows that the private R&D environment in business in Northern Ireland is one of fairly substantial but falling public subsidy through direct grants and tax deductions, with average grant rates of between 30 and 50 per cent[93]. The level of industrial R&D in Northern Ireland has increased substantially in the 1990s under this regime. However, despite this success, Government financial support for industrial R&D in Northern Ireland needs to be

---

[92]   *These data are from NIEC (1999b). They refer to the value of offers accepted by companies and universities in a given year. The offer will typically be disbursed over several years. The values reported are in 1995-96£. The data are drawn from IRTU's Annual Report.*

[93]   *For more detail, see NIEC (1999b).*

assessed. As OECD (1998a) notes, there has been in the OECD a "recent shift in innovation policies from direct support of R&D to measures which increase the adoptive capabilities of firms and improve the framework conditions in which they operate" (p.24). What this means is that emphasis must increasingly be on building university, Government and business partnerships and improving the regional R&D system, rather than on giving grants to companies to do their own R&D, although efforts to raise private R&D spending in the economy must continue. This has not to date been taken far in Northern Ireland, as IRTU past and projected grant levels to companies indicate.

8.19   One aspect of the grants and assistance for R&D strategy in Northern Ireland that requires attention is the sometimes confusing plethora of grants and schemes available, from primarily IRTU, but also from other agencies such as NIGC, IDB and LEDU[94]. Much of this of course reflects the different sources of funds, such as EU Framework and Structural, IFI, DTI and Northern Ireland Government funds, as well as the differing goals and priorities of different funds, such as mission-oriented project finance, diffusion-oriented technical support and transfer, and technical personnel assistance. Thus, it could be argued that there is a need to integrate all R&D support, especially for SMEs. One option would be a 'One Stop Shop' or single point of contact, co-ordinated by DED, and involving the various agencies and partnerships.

Intermural Department Expenditure

8.20   Despite some notable successes in selected areas, Government departments in Northern Ireland do not appear to co-operate and collaborate to the extent demanded in the R&D environment of the knowledge-based economy. There are good examples of collaboration

---

[94] *NIGC provides no financial assistance for R&D but does co-ordinate activity on Foresight. The IDB provides not R&D grants but assistance for employment in R&D establishments.*

(eg IRTU and DANI in the food group industries, IRTU and DENI through their representation on the NIHEC Research Committee and hence consultation on NIDevR funds) but these appear to be the exceptions that prove the rule. Existing IDCs seem to be loose and informal, such that there is little advance knowledge between Departments as to what each is doing in R&D. What knowledge there is appears to be shared more after the event rather than in planning co-ordinated efforts in R&D. A notable exception is the DANI/DoE (NI) Scientific Liaison Committee, which involves the departments working closely together on an ongoing basis.

8.21   The review of departmental S&T expenditure in the UK, mentioned in Section 6 above, the so-called Boundaries Review, notes much Northern Ireland Department involvement in co-ordination of R&D with their UK Department counterparts, on specific issues. This is especially true of DANI but much less so of DoE (NI). The review concluded that Northern Ireland Departments, especially DoE (NI), but also presumably DED, were not as fully engaged with GB departments such as the then DOT, DoE[95] and DTI, on issues such as transport, the environment, and energy. It could be argued that the R&D spend in DoE (NI) is perhaps too low, and appears to be an identifiable gap in the Northern Ireland system, where additional investment might be beneficial.

8.22   Technology transfer and commercialisation of R&D from Government Departments appears to be limited. For example, DANI research might be crowding out industry research and acting as substitute rather than a complement to it[96]. Of 274 DANI research projects ongoing in 1997-98, only 14 were partially commercially funded (4 out of 100 in crop, grain and livestock production, 7 out of 99 in animal health and

---

95   *DOT and DoE were amalgamated in 1996-97 to form the Department of Environment, Transport and the Regions (DETR).*

96   *However, the DANI/QUB link does allow for industry funding of research in the agri-food sector, as evidenced by the £2.7m per annum in DANI research contracts.*

welfare, food quality, processing and safety, and 3 out of 75 in fisheries, environmental management, economic and rural development, and forestry). In 1996-97, 234 academic papers were produced from the research programme, an average of 2.3 per academic researcher, but a lack of jointly-funded industry-Government-university research is apparent[97]. Food and food processing is a large and important industrial sector in Northern Ireland but little research is undertaken outside DANI and, despite substantial impacts that have been achieved in the local agri-food sector through technology transfer from DANI research, there is no evidence of a food technology cluster. There is, however, the Agri-food Development Service (AFDS) of DANI, and Loughry College in Cookstown has 'incubators' for commercialisation and technology transfer. IRTU also funds business R&D in food and food processing and there is cross-membership between DANI and IRTU on their Food Management Board. A proposal currently under consideration is the establishment of a Northern Ireland Food Technology Foresight Centre as a mechanism for technology transfer into the agri-food sector.

8.23   A major problem is the lack of a mechanism for ongoing monitoring and appraisal of overall Government Department activities, and for revision of emphasis in response to changing needs and opportunities. Department budgets in recent years have been cut on a crude 'across the board' basis as a result of the CSR, and there is no mechanism for flexible changing in commitments and allocations, and no provision for increased intramural departmental spending over the next three years (Table 8.2 and Figure 8C). Some R&D, such as on environmental issues, appears to be under-funded relative to other programmes, such as DANI. The dominance of DANI in the share of Department activity suggests either a lack of attention to R&D in the

---

[97] *Of course, all Government departments, including DANI, are primarily in the business of policy, not providing consultancy services to business.*

other Departments, or over-specialisation in agricultural research[98]. Moreover, one does not get the sense that departmental R&D programmes in Northern Ireland are of sufficient flexibility to constitute, for example, an evolving strategic development of research in biotechnology, forecast to be a major technological area of the future, even though the agri-food R&D area is one where there does appear to be a good degree of co-ordination in Northern Ireland. Overall, it does not appear that departmental R&D budgets are sufficiently flexible, both within and between Departments, to respond to changing economic and social needs and priorities.

The Health R&D Programme

8.24   R&D in health is about better health care provision, and not about economic development per se. Benefits must be considered in terms of health and social indicators, not economic ones. There is, however, strong evidence of positive association between better health and social conditions and improved economic competitiveness and performance. Moreover, as stated in the HPSS R&D Strategy document;

> R&D of relevance to health and social care does not necessarily generate commercially-exploitable know-ledge, but increasingly co-operation with industry leads to such economic spin-offs (HPSS, 1999, p.11).

8.25   It will be important that the R&D strategy of HPSS as it evolves redistributes funding away from relatively weak areas of R&D in Northern Ireland and towards relative strengths and strategic priorities. A major task of the Strategy will be to balance relevance, quality and critical

---

98   *DANI's intramural research programme is, however, not solely targeted on agricultural research, with programmes in place on Environmental Management, Food Safety, Food Quality and Processing, Fisheries and their Environment, Forestry, Horticulture, and Economics and Rural Development.*

mass, through focus, selectivity and coherence. Another will be to increase capacity and capability in health and social care research, through research groups, education and training and career development (HPSS, 1999). It was, however, unfortunate that the HPSS R&D budget for 1998-99 and 1999-2000 (Table 8.2), was set well below the level of expenditure estimated in 1996-97 and 1997-98 of approximately £12-£14m.

8.26   The private sector is perhaps not integrated enough into R&D in the health services in Northern Ireland. Public-private partnerships should be encouraged as the next step in the process of prioritising R&D in the HPSS begun by the Culyer declarations of non-commercial R&D activities and expenditures, and the establishment of the HPSS R&D Office. A possibility exists of establishing a clinical trials centre on a public-private partnership. Special initiatives to develop R&D infrastructure and activity in specific areas (such as in the primary and community sectors and in social care) should also be built on partnership approaches. However, the RDO is in its early days and the move to co-ordinate and to raise the profile of R&D to one of being a core activity in the HPSS is to be welcomed and is perhaps a model for the other Government Departments to follow.

The University R&D Programme

8.27   There is in the OECD a trend in R&D of a shift away from basic research towards market-driven science and technology development efforts. OECD (1998a) states "Increased efficiency in R&D, or a greater applied focus, may well outweigh the short-term effects of reduced basic R&D. However, such an offsetting effect is less likely in the long-run" (p.98). In other words, a declining attention to basic research may improve competitiveness in the short-run, but erode it in the long run. It is important that a correct balance of basic and applied research is struck. OECD, as noted in Box 2 above, stresses that there must be adequate public financing of basic research.

8.28   There are indicators to suggest that expenditure on R&D in universities in Northern Ireland, where the vast bulk of basic research in the region is undertaken, is low relative to other regions of the UK and elsewhere, and Figure 8B, above, shows that block funding is projected to fall in Northern Ireland in real per capita terms, but rise in the rest of the UK, to 2001-02. Figure 8D shows that funding from the higher education

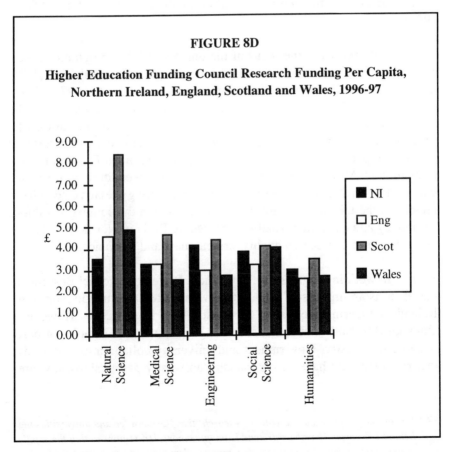

FIGURE 8D

Higher Education Funding Council Research Funding Per Capita, Northern Ireland, England, Scotland and Wales, 1996-97

Source: DTI/ONS (1998, p.44)

147

funding bodies for Northern Ireland, England, Scotland and Wales are broadly similar on a per capita basis across the disciplines. However, this block funding makes up over 50 per cent of all funding to Northern Ireland universities but less than 40 per cent for the GB universities. It has been estimated that if total research expenditure in universities in Northern Ireland per head of population was to be brought up to the UK average level, an additional £20m in funds, from either the public or private sector or both, would be required by the two universities (SQW, 1997)[99].

8.29   With regard to the focus of the university R&D programme, the approach of UU to specialisation has been strategic, whereas that of QUB has been diverse, but becoming more specialised (QUB, 1997). The universities wish to retain their autonomy and independence on R&D strategy but there is an obvious need for strategic co-ordination of programme spending between the universities, Government and industry. It is also important that close attention to the quality of R&D is continued through the RAE and other processes. However, expenditure on R&D in universities in Northern Ireland is low and falling (relative to other regions in the UK) and this must be rectified within the context of value-for-money and economic benefit of university R&D in Northern Ireland, using measures of research quality, critical mass and relevance.

8.30   In work in progress for the Council, Professor Michael Best finds that there is an impressive range of university R&D centres in Northern Ireland, numbering more than 25 (Best, 1999, in process). However, although Best finds that some, such as QUESTOR, are examples of best practice in industry, Government and university collaboration, he finds that relatively few have active industry/university partnerships, few are

---

[99]   *It is not just in knowledge creation (research) that Northern Ireland universities lag behind UK norms. Northern Ireland is unique among UK regions in that the supply of university student places is less than regional demand, and hence Northern Ireland universities also lag in knowledge transmission.*

integrated with the technological change processes of entrepreneurial firms, and most are highly under-utilised by Government and business. He also notes that there is potential for collaboration between companies and colleges of further education in Northern Ireland, but that this potential is presently unmet. However, the Teaching Company Scheme and College Business Partnership are successful approaches to academic-business collaboration and co-operation[100].

8.31   As noted in *Strategy 2010*, greater integration of economic and educational policy is required with economic development strategy informing education and training policy and its funding and delivery mechanisms, and with more resources for university-business collaboration (Economic Development Strategy Review Steering Group, 1999). The release of proposals for a Higher Education Reach-out to Business and the Community Fund by the HEFCE in March 1999, is hence to be welcomed (HEFCE, 1999).

Conclusion

8.32   What then are the answers to the questions posed in the introduction to this section and to the report? In the absence of specific evidence on outputs or impacts of the public R&D spend in Northern Ireland, it is of course impossible to determine whether maximum economic benefit is being derived from it, although there is evidence that innovation levels are low in the economy (Roper and Hewitt-Dundas, 1998). We have tried to point out some gaps where additional investment might be beneficial, for example, in university R&D, in support for SMEs, and in environment issues. With regard to duplication and overlap, these are guaranteed to exist given the complex and interdisciplinary nature of the modern R&D process, and should not necessarily be viewed as problematic. They do, however, demonstrate the

---

100   *It is important to note that the approximately £2m expenditure by the universities on TCS is not included in the figures for university R&D presented above in section 4.*

need for co-ordination, collaboration and collective effort, across and between the main publicly funded programmes and between public and private R&D. The level of funding and policy priority given to R&D and the level of co-ordination of R&D in Northern Ireland is sub-optimal, with the region lacking a comprehensive and inclusive R&D and innovation strategy. Northern Ireland does not bench-mark well against other regions, and *Strategy 2010* does not go far enough in these respects. Moreover, although not all of it is suitable for such purposes, publicly funded R&D in Northern Ireland is inadequately channelled to commercialisation, and inadequately integrated into overall economic development strategy. A more balanced and focused knowledge management strategy within the context of economic development policy is needed to translate publicly and privately funded R&D activity into maximum economic and social benefit. Although the efficiency of public and private R&D spending (how well they channel to public and private innovation) is becoming more important to economic development than the size of public and private R&D budgets, attention in Northern Ireland must also be given to increasing existing low levels of public and private R&D in an appropriately balanced way, and to increasing the funding and policy priority given to public and private R&D and innovation, within the context of an economic development strategy.

9 CONCLUSIONS AND RECOMMENDATIONS FOR POLICY

Introduction

9.1   It is the Council's view that investment in R&D and innovation in Northern Ireland is a critical determinant of enduring competitiveness. Raising the profile of R&D and innovation in Government, health, education and industry, strengthening the R&D base of the two local universities, providing better links between the major agents responsible for producing R&D, and using it through technology transfer and innovation, should be the major priority items in economic development strategy in Northern Ireland.

9.2   The major conclusion of this report is that the publicly funded R&D system in Northern Ireland is not currently being prioritised and co-ordinated to achieve maximum economic benefit. R&D, both public and private, is too low, both in absolute terms and relative to Northern Ireland's major economic competitors, and publicly funded R&D is not being adequately channelled to commercial exploitation and to economic development. There exist some excellent R&D capabilities in Northern Ireland but, due to an inadequate level of co-ordination and co-operation between Government, industry, the universities and other stakeholders, these capabilities are not being exploited to their maximum economic potential. In this concluding section therefore we move on to the last three questions posed in the introduction to this report and which so far remain unanswered, namely:

- How might Government in Northern Ireland revise and develop its publicly funded R&D programmes to be better directed at innovation and competitiveness and at extracting maximum economic benefit in Northern Ireland?

- How might better co-ordination of R&D spending and programme delivery between Government Departments, agencies, universities and business in Northern Ireland be secured?

151

- Is there a need for new institutions or mechanisms for strategic R&D funding and policy co-ordination in Northern Ireland, or for a new minister, office or agency with overall remit for regional R&D strategy and policy?

The recommendations contained in the remainder of this report are devoted to providing answers to these questions. We offer recommendations in relation to the five major constituent themes or policy areas of the public R&D spend in Northern Ireland discussed in Sections 7 and 8 above; overall co-ordination, networking and linkages, grants and assistance to R&D, intramural Department expenditure, the health programme, and the university programme. We begin with recommendations regarding the overall co-ordination of publicly funded R&D policy and strategy in Northern Ireland.

Overall Co-ordination, Networking and Linkages

A Central Co-ordinating Institution

9.3   No institution in Northern Ireland is currently addressing the major issues of this report involving the co-ordination of the public R&D spend with private spending to achieve maximum economic benefit. Such a remit is well beyond the current activities of IRTU. What is required is a central unit (IRTU or otherwise) with budgetary responsibility ranging over the entirety of the public spend and with a knowledge management remit similar to that found in institutions in other jurisdictions such as those examined in Section 6 above. Thus,

> the Council recommends that a single institution or unit of Government should have responsibility for overall co-ordination of R&D policy and budgetary responsibility for R&D in Northern Ireland.

The possible form of the institution is discussed further below and will draw on the discussion in Section 6.

9.4   In order to achieve maximum benefit from the public spend, a number of major issues will need to be addressed. Thus,

the Council <u>recommends</u> that the remit of the single institution or unit within Government with overall responsibility for R&D in Northern Ireland should include:

- an overview of the R&D programme, the scrutiny of overlap, gaps, crowding-out and duplication, and the exploitation of potential for co-ordination and synergy, including the co-ordination of cross-departmental issues;

- monitoring and adjustment of the allocation of R&D resources across Government Departments, R&D grants and assistance, the university programme, and the health programme, and the sharing of good practice between programmes;

- monitoring of quality, focus, selectivity, critical mass and cost-effectiveness in programmes, including measurement of social and economic benefit impacts;

- the allocation of additional public funding for public and private R&D programmes, including sources of funds for industry-academic links;

- the encouragement and measurement of commercial exploitation of publicly funded R&D in Northern Ireland including spin-out companies; and,

- the design of a Northern Ireland R&D and innovation strategy to meet the needs of a knowledge-based economy, with balanced, phased and realistic targets for public and private R&D and innovation.

Successful management of such a remit, within the context of overall Government strategy and public expenditure decisions, would better co-ordinate public and private R&D spending in Northern Ireland and go a considerable way towards ensuring maximum economic and social benefit from public and private R&D. It would allow Government to more fully carry out its role in knowledge management for economic development discussed in Section 3 above - of building networks and connections and resolving systemic failures in knowledge creation and its channelling to economic and social benefit. In many ways the regional remit would be similar to that carried out by the OST at the UK national level. It will however require various institutional mechanisms in order to ensure that the remit will not wither on the vine.

9.5   There are many possible options regarding the institutional arrangements through which the central co-ordination of the overall R&D spend can be effected. There must be an overview of the various strands of publicly funded R&D activity and they must be joined up under a central unit of Government and within a regional R&D and innovation strategy. Strategic thinking and concerted action is required to move publicly funded R&D forward so that the stretching targets for Northern Ireland economic performance being set by the Government, most recently in the DED draft economic development strategy document, *Strategy 2010*, can be achieved. Although precise institutional arrangements are an issue secondary to that of effecting central co-ordination, we present a possible institutional template after we have considered other related issues.

An Annual Survey of R&D and Innovation

9.6   For a central co-ordinating institution to operate effectively, reliable and up-to-date information will be required. It is important that the inconsistencies in the reporting of R&D expenditure in Northern Ireland, as shown in Section 4, are overcome. Close attention to R&D and innovation data is needed, with accurate and consistent surveying, accounting and reporting of annual estimates of R&D and innovation activity in the economy. Thus,

> the Council <u>recommends</u> that an annual survey of R&D
> and innovation in the economy, inclusive of university
> activity, should be commissioned.

The current tri-annual R&D survey of the DED should fully integrate with the ONS annual survey and include the universities' expenditures and activities[101]. The survey should also be expanded to include innovation activities.

An Annual R&D and Innovation Budget

9.7   Reliable information on the total amount of public funding will also be required. As earlier sections of this report have shown, this is a complex field both statistically and institutionally. Thus,

> the Council <u>recommends</u> that an Annual R&D and
> Innovation Budget and a Single Programme of publicly
> funded R&D and innovation activities, goals and
> priorities should be consolidated, set and monitored.

---

101   *There are new proposals on accounting for university R&D through the DTI which will help in estimating university activity ("DTI to scrutinise all spending" <u>Time Higher Education Supplement</u>, June 18, 1999). Any proposed Tertiary Sector Funding Council could also develop accounting methods in this area.*

Given that the Northern Ireland R&D and innovation system involves Government, industry and university collaboration, the idea of the publication of not only an annual R&D and Innovation Budget, but also, the consolidation of all initiatives into a Single Programme of public funding for R&D and innovation activities, wherever they are undertaken, in Government, in industry or in the universities, should be considered, co-ordinated through the central co-ordinating institution in co-operation with the various funding bodies. A single programme would allow for synergies to be more readily identified and exploited, would provide transparency in the allocation of public resources for R&D, and would allow a better balance to be struck between public basic and strategic R&D and support for private sector R&D.

An R&D and Innovation Strategy

9.8   It is vital that Northern Ireland has an R&D and innovation strategy, given the close connections between R&D, innovation, and economic performance. Thus,

> the Council recommends that a co-ordinated R&D and Innovation Strategy should be developed for Northern Ireland with phased and balanced targets for both public and private R&D and innovation.

This should be developed by the institution charged with overall R&D funding and policy responsibility in co-operation with Government departments, the universities, and business. It should use available European regional expertise and experience in RIS/RITTS development, with an ultimate goal of mainstreaming and embedding R&D and Innovation strategy into overall economic development strategy. A knowledge economy task force could provide a realistic assessment of Northern Ireland's R&D and innovation capabilities in order to begin to build upon them - with an immediate goal of coming to an assessment of R&D innovation capabilities in the economy, across business,

Government and the universities, and a medium-term goal of becoming the basis for an R&D and innovation strategy for Northern Ireland. Northern Ireland could benefit from implementing what has worked well in other EU regions in the process of creating inputs and reaching consensus in RIS/RITTS and on following through into quantifiable outputs.

9.9   *Strategy 2010* calls for business spending on R&D of 1.5 per cent of GDP by 2010 but has no targets for Government, university and other public institutional spending on R&D. There must, however, be a balanced, co-ordinated and increased commitment to public as well as private R&D and innovation in Northern Ireland. To meet *Strategy 2010's* target for business expenditure, and to be consistent with *Strategy 2010's* target for GDP (ie to be 90 per cent of the UK per capita average by 2010), private business expenditure on R&D would have to grow in real terms by about 15 per cent per year to 2010[102]. If it did so, and if public R&D expenditure stayed at its current level (£80m or so), private business R&D would grow from about 50 per cent of all R&D expenditure to 80 per cent, the public contribution falling from 50 per cent to 20 per cent[103]. This public contribution would be far below current UK, EU and OECD national and regional averages[104]. Hence, some thought must be given to establishing phased and balanced targets for both public and private R&D, and for encouraging innovation in not just the private sector but in the public sector also. R&D and innovation need encouragement in universities, Government departments and NDPBs (eg the health service), as well as in industry. Moreover, R&D is a cross-

---

102   *GDP in Northern Ireland would have to grow by about 4.5 per cent per year in real terms, 2000-2010, to about £2.4bn in 2010, and hence private business expenditure on R&D would have to grow from its current level of around £80m to £360m in 2010 (1.5 per cent of £2.4bn), or by around 15 per cent per year in real terms. It grew by 9 per cent per year in real terms, 1993 to 1996.*

103   *Total R&D would rise to £420m or 1.75 per cent of GDP in 2010.*

104   *See Section 5.*

cutting social and economic issue that must be co-ordinated.

9.10   Given the experience of regions of similar economic size discussed in Section 6, a Northern Ireland R&D and innovation strategy might best be structured on sectoral lines, to best integrate and co-ordinate Government, business and university R&D for innovation and economic development. A sectoral approach could foster public-private partnership and co-operation and improve the effectiveness of the public spend in increasing private sector R&D activity.   Such a strategy could best balance R&D in each sector between mission-oriented research, where scale and critical mass in research consortia are important, and diffusion-oriented activities, such as quality improvement and technical personnel assistance. A sectoral strategy might lead to the development of public-private research institutions and directorates and help direct public R&D towards industrial competitiveness goals. One approach could be to build on industry-academic links, as is currently being emphasised in regions such as Scotland, Wales, Yorkshire and Humberside and the North East, and as has been taken some way in Northern Ireland already through IRTU and the universities.

9.11   A question to be addressed is which sector should be included in a sectorally based strategy. Specific sectoral measures for publicly funded R&D, subject to conclusions of the Northern Ireland Foresight Panels, might be considered in ICT[105] (in collaboration with the proposed Information Age Commission), in Biotechnology and Food Technology[106] (in collaboration with DANI and the HPSS) and in

---

[105] *ICT is an underlying and enabling technology for society in general and business in particular. US estimates claim that fully one-third of all economic growth in the last decade has been due to ICT (Technology Foresight Ireland, 1999, p.38).*

[106] *It is argued that biotechnology is going to reveal more knowledge in the coming decades than all other technologies combined, and will be to the early twenty-first century what physics and chemistry were to the mid-twentieth (Technology Foresight Ireland, 1999, p.39).*

Sustainable Development and Environment (in collaboration with DANI and DoE (NI)). The Northern Ireland Software Industry Federation has recently argued for a focused strategy for its sector based on R&D and innovation (SIF, 1999). All sectors of the economy, public and private, tradable or non-tradable, manufacturing or services, would benefit from a sectoral R&D and innovation strategy, not just those of the newer and higher technologies, given the strong linkages between sectors. An additional focus could be on clusters development and management which would require attention to all sectors of the economy. However, the small size of the Northern Ireland economy might limit the scope for cluster-based strategy.

9.12   Given the small size of most sectors in the Northern Ireland economy, a sectoral R&D and innovation strategy would inevitably come down to targeting specific firms for support. Although the small cadre of large, foreign-owned firms and their linkages with the local economy will often appear to be the most obvious candidate for support, attention must also be given to indigenous SMEs which are high value-added, growth and export oriented. Support for research-intensive multinational corporations should form only one component of a sectoral or clusters development strategy which provides generalised support for industrial improvement and diffusion of best practice. In developing a sectoral R&D and innovation strategy for Northern Ireland, the experience of RIS/RITTS activities so far conducted in other regions of Europe could be taken on board, with their focus on the needs of regional SMEs. Many of these, however, were strong on inputs and consensus but weak on outputs and follow through, and Northern Ireland could learn in this regard from others. The focus in Northern Ireland might best be on specific, agreed sectoral projects for mission-oriented R&D and targets for R&D diffusion and innovation, based on diffusion of academic R&D and its commercial exploitation by local SMEs.

9.13   Some attention would also have to be given to the phasing in of strategy. It would be difficult to do everything right away.

Implementation of the strategy might begin in areas where the maximum economic benefit can be leveraged at the least cost, and then move on to more difficult areas. For example, implementation might begin with diffusion of knowledge and industry-academic links from foreign direct investment, through a Regional Linkages Initiative recommended recently in a Council report on linkages and foreign direct investment (NIEC, 1999a). It might then move on to knowledge networking with indigenous companies, first large, and then small and medium-sized. Proposals to develop the science base could follow, focusing on R&D capabilities first and then on their exploitation for economic benefit. Again, where the appropriate starting points for building R&D and innovation strategy should be, and where that strategy should then move on to, could be informed by the experiences of the regions discussed in Section 6 above and by the EU RIS/RITTS regions.

North-South Co-ordination

9.14   North-South collaboration in the areas of R&D, S&T and innovation should be encouraged as part of Northern Ireland R&D and innovation strategy. For example, Foresight might be pursued on an all-Ireland basis, and joint S&T awareness campaigns along the lines of a Science Week in Ireland could be created. Certainly, initiatives for the universities to collaborate in research on an all-Ireland basis should be encouraged. Now that Foresight is fully operational in the RoI, North-South collaboration might be the best way to move forward with the Northern Ireland Foresight programme. Moreover, opportunities exist in formulating Single Programming Documents to mainstream and co-ordinate EU R&D and innovation initiatives North and South. In Section 7 existing North-South initiatives are described and,

> the Council recommends that North-South collaboration
> in R&D and innovation should be encouraged as part of
> a Northern Ireland R&D and innovation strategy.

Furthermore, as shown in Section 6, RoI has made a number of moves to raise the profile of R&D and innovation from which Northern Ireland might learn.

A Knowledge-Driven Economic Development Strategy

9.15   It is increasingly important that economic development in Northern Ireland be innovation and knowledge-driven. The development of an R&D and innovation strategy would enable overall economic development strategy in Northern Ireland to reflect the innovation imperative, as it does in the UK (with the release of the 1998 Competitiveness White Paper). Government in Northern Ireland must pursue, in partnership with the universities and industry, a knowledge-led economic development strategy that has as its goal the enhancement of the technology management and innovative capabilities of the most promising and progressive firms and other public and private productive organisations in Northern Ireland. Thus, in order to encourage a holistic approach to R&D, innovation and economic development strategy,

> the Council <u>recommends</u> that the R&D and Innovation Strategy developed for Northern Ireland be fully embedded into a knowledge-driven economic development strategy.

9.16   The economic development strategies of the other regions of the UK appear to be more coherently based on the knowledge-driven economy than *Strategy 2010*. For example, as in Scotland, the critical players in the regional knowledge-driven economy and the regional R&D and innovation system, especially the regional universities and indigenous industries, but also international public and private R&D and innovation partners, must be prominently represented in the design and implementation of economic development strategy.

Grants and Assistance to R&D

9.17   In recent considerations of public expenditure on economic development in Northern Ireland, the Council has argued for, among other things, increased public investment in technological development and the promotion of R&D[107]. The recently published economic development strategy for Northern Ireland, *Strategy 2010,* calls for business spending on R&D of 1.5 per cent of GDP by 2010. Such a target is ambitious and, to achieve it, grants to business in Northern Ireland must shift from subsidising the production of goods and services to encouraging the production and management of knowledge. Moreover, grants should not be a subsidy for business R&D in general, but be tied to building long-term R&D capability in firms committed to knowledge creation and management as a long-term strategy for their growth, and based more on improving the knowledge infrastructure in which firms operate, as argued in Section 8. Focus should especially be on SMEs and new R&D performers, with emphasis on co-operation and collaboration with other firms[108], and with universities and Government[109]. Targets for increased public R&D also need to be set to support such substantial increases in private business R&D. Whatever the specific policy initiatives, there must be an increased public commitment to both private and public R&D and innovation in Northern Ireland. Thus,

> the Council recommends that increased public expenditure should be committed to the encouragement in an appropriately balanced way of both private and

---

[107]   *NIEC (1997, pp.52-54), and NIEC (1999b).*

[108]   *However, every attempt should be made to ensure that rigorous tests for dead-weight and displacement are undertaken. The emphasis on co-operation/collaboration should be designed to maximise technological transfer.*

[109]   *The Northern Ireland Software Industry Federation has recently recommended that IRTU should allocate a minimum annual budget of £10m to software R&D (SIF, 1999).*

public R&D and innovation in Northern Ireland, based on a long-term capabilities-building and public-private partnership approach.

9.18   This increased public commitment would be within the remit of the central co-ordinating institution or unit. In order to shift grants away from subsidy and towards capability building, it will be required that the unit undertake a comprehensive audit and assessment of the R&D, innovation and knowledge management capabilities of Northern Ireland firms, universities and Government departments and agencies and other public and private institutions. Such an audit would expose what the critical infrastructural needs of Northern Ireland firms and other public and private institutions are, in relation to knowledge networks, R&D, innovation and economic development. Funds should then be targeted at those firms and organisations with the most promising long-term potential for entrepreneurship and for growth around knowledge management and innovation.

9.19   Renewed and special emphasis is required to promote R&D in SMEs, given the predominantly SME nature of the Northern Ireland economy. A focus on new R&D performers would help here, and a proposed single economic development agency with priority for R&D, innovation and SMEs might ensure closer co-operation between the initiatives and endeavours of the current IDB, LEDU, IRTU and Training and Employment Agency (T&EA). Enhanced support for innovation in SMEs could then be contemplated, with perhaps free consultancy to SMEs on innovation, subsidies for employing scientists and engineers, and access to a Knowledge House or Bridge, perhaps building on the Manufacturing Technology Partnership initiatives described in Section 7.

9.20   Government funds might be well spent in encouraging the public and private research and knowledge producers, including the universities and the further education colleges, to establish, in co-operation, technology transfer and support networks such as the Knowledge Houses,

Bridges and Know How Centres found in some other regions and noted in Section 6. Such practical networks are useful 'one stop shops' for companies in search of technology support and assistance, especially SMEs. Certainly, such 'spin-in' networks could usefully supplement the Science Park initiative and new university initiatives in the commercialisation of their research through spin-out enterprises. Such a network would allow the colleges and universities to increase their contribution to job and wealth creation in Northern Ireland, and could be a joint education and economic development (DED/DENI) initiative. Thus,

> the Council <u>recommends</u> that a regional Knowledge Bridge for technology transfer and support between Government, universities, higher and further education colleges, and SMEs should be established.

Intramural Department Expenditure

9.21   The present allocation of R&D across departments needs to be reviewed as to its emphasis and effectiveness. R&D is a cross-departmental issue that must be co-ordinated so as to ensure priorities set are operationalised. Departments undertake much of their research in support of their department's policy, statutory, operational, regulatory and procurement responsibilities, but much can be better co-ordinated with attention to priority-setting. Certainly, prioritising is necessary when additional spending across the whole system is being contemplated, as it is here. Since total public funding of R&D is about one per cent of the Northern Ireland Government budget[110], and per capita Government-funding of R&D activity in Northern Ireland is below average UK levels (Figure 8A), there is no reason why R&D should not be at least one or two per cent of the total budget of each Department. These percentages

---

[110] *Public funding of R&D amounted to £79m in 1996; total appropriations for Northern Ireland were around £8bn.*

are currently much exceeded by DANI (£8m, or 5 per cent, to R&D in a budget of around £170m) but are much above current levels of R&D in the other Departments[111].

9.22   An institution with an overall co-ordination remit and budgetary responsibility for public R&D spending could decide where additional funds for departmental research and its commercialisation should be allocated and competitively distributed on the basis of departmental applications and priorities set by Foresight and other mechanisms. Greater competition for research funds could be promoted, on the basis of multi-year research strategies of the departments tied to regional priorities, for example, on environmental issues, sustainable development, the rational management of natural resources, food technology and ICT. Greater collaboration of R&D and innovation between Departments, NDPBs, universities and industry could also be promoted by these R&D plans and research strategies, which could be revised and refocused every three or four years, based on evolving social and economic development needs, with annual priority setting and evaluation and monitoring as to impact and the meeting of objectives on a regular basis. A strategic R&D and innovation fund for these purposes could be established using existing departmental appropriations and matching such funds with additional resources, for reallocation based on competitive application. Such a fund could help ensure that departmental R&D activities would not become inflexibly fossilised in recurring and fixed annual appropriations, but instead continuously revised in response to changing priorities and co-ordinated with outside R&D and innovation activities. Under Devolution the establishment of ten Departments or other arrangements would provide both the opportunity and the increased need to establish such co-ordination. Thus,

---

111   *DANI themselves (rather than ONS) quote R&D expenditure figures of £6m in 1996/97 and £5.3m in 1997/98, which represent closer to 3 per cent rather than 5 per cent of the DANI budget.*

the Council <u>recommends</u> that intramural Department R&D expenditure should be better prioritised and co-ordinated and that a strategic R&D and Innovation Fund be established for public funding of collaborative R&D and innovation between departments, NDPBs, universities and industry.

The Health R&D Programme

9.23   The Council endorses the recommendations of the HPSS R&D Strategy published in April 1999 (HPSS, 1999), especially the need to co-ordinate the overall R&D spend in HPSS and to fully engage the universities in the health R&D strategy. The R&D office of HPSS can act as a model for other Departments in co-ordinating and centralising their R&D function. As the HPSS R&D Strategy evolves, it will be important to encourage commercial exploitation of R&D results, especially in health care products such as health informatics and those involving indigenous threshold SMEs.   In many countries Government and the health authorities work closely with indigenous companies to develop world class products and help these companies gain world scale. Pilot projects in the Life and Health Technologies field involving Government, the health authorities and the NIGC should be encouraged. There is, for example, an existing proposal for a medical informatics incubator at the proposed Springvale campus (SIF, 1999). Therefore,

the Council <u>recommends</u> that R&D in Northern Ireland, including health sector R&D, should be exploited for maximum economic benefit in Northern Ireland.

The University R&D Programme

9.24   In order to build up the R&D capabilities of Northern Ireland, the means to address the recent decline in the core funding of the research base in the universities must be considered. Block funding for research in

Northern Ireland universities has fallen over the last few years, and is forecast to continue to fall to 2001-2002, in contrast to a rising trend in the rest of the UK (Figure 8B above). The Council was, therefore, critical of the reduction in research support for universities of £4m in the 1996 Public Expenditure Survey (PES) which saw Northern Ireland lag behind the rest of the UK (Figure 4A). The budget for research students was also cut. The Council's concern was reinforced by the National Committee of Inquiry into Higher Education (NCIHE) report that emphasised the importance of university R&D in Northern Ireland due to "the structure of the economy, with its small firms, the prevalence of external ownership and bias towards low-technology operations, [that] reduces the short-term opportunities for research conducted by business" (NCIHE, 1997, p.455). The two universities in Northern Ireland are the two largest single components of the regional R&D system and they have critical roles to play in R&D innovation and economic development. Therefore, given the importance of strong local universities to regional economic strategy and the potential contribution of the universities to that strategy,

> the Council recommends that block funding for university research in Northern Ireland should be increased so as to reinforce R&D and innovation links between universities, Government and industry.

Block funding for Northern Ireland universities would have to be £8.5m more than planned to reach UK average per capita levels in 2001-02.

9.25   An increased commitment to university research outside the block is also required along with increased university input into regional economic development based on knowledge creation and commercialisation. New sources of funds for industry-academic links and funding for research in the universities making adequate provision for funding based on Northern Ireland's social and economic needs would help to better co-ordinate public and private R&D spending in Northern Ireland. A major review of the RAE is scheduled to begin in 2000 involving the universities, the OST, and representatives of research users such as the CBI (OST, 1999, p.53). This will inform funding methodologies from 2004 onwards, after those set by RAE 2001. It will be important that Northern Ireland input emphasises the need to give appropriate recognition to both basic and applied research of quality and relevance to the needs of the local economy. There is concern, often expressed in many quarters, that the current RAE funding criteria are somewhat biased against useful local applied research.

9.26   If there is to be an increased commitment to university R&D above that necessary to bring funding for university research in Northern Ireland closer to the average UK per capita level, a substantial portion of these increased funds could perhaps be allocated through the central co-ordinating institution recommended above and based on university-industry joint ventures, leveraging equivalent amounts of private finance. Other approaches might be to allocate through a Tertiary Sector Funding Council (TSFC) (DENI, 1999), for the economic development agencies to match new funds from the third leg of funding of the new Reach Out initiative, or for the Reach Out funds themselves to be increased. Given the increasing importance of university interaction with public agencies and business alongside their traditional roles of teaching and research, new sources of funds for industry-academic links must be considered, as is the case in Scotland (Scottish Office, 1999). The Northern Ireland universities might then be able to be full partners with their GB counterparts in knowledge creation (research), transmission (teaching and training) and transfer to the economy. Thus,

> the Council recommends that new approaches to university research funding should be established through the funding bodies and the economic development agencies to increase the relevance of university R&D to the local economy.

9.27   Although IRTU does encourage industry-academic links in its administration of R&D grants, there is perhaps a need to channel more grants to businesses through universities and research institutions and agencies in collaboration with business, rather than through direct subsidies to industry alone. The universities in Northern Ireland are a critical source of new knowledge and consequently have an opportunity and a responsibility to become engines of regional economic growth. R&D, innovation and economic development strategy should be added to their arsenal along with their existing commitments to teaching and research. As noted by the study completed for the Dearing Report (NCIHE, 1997) on Higher Education and Regions: "In an increasingly competitive global economy there is an evident need to develop higher-level skills, to make provision for lifetime retraining and to capitalise on the application of research findings in product and process innovations. Universities represent a considerable resource to address these challenges, but it is a resource that is as yet under exploited" (Robson et al, 1997, p.186). For example, in revising funding for research in the Northern Ireland universities, adequate provision should be made for funding outside DENI and NIHEC block funding and for Foresight and other special initiatives based on Northern Ireland R&D needs and innovation.

A Possible Institutional Arrangement

Central Co-ordinating Institution

9.28   As argued above, the effective management of knowledge creation and utilisation in the Northern Ireland economy requires the focused attention of a dedicated unit of Government. Such a unit could closely monitor R&D, S&T and innovation in Northern Ireland and how Northern Ireland can be linked to other knowledge pools at home and abroad. This institution or unit, as discussed above, would have responsibility for:

•   R&D and innovation surveying, monitoring and reporting;

- R&D and innovation budget and single programme setting and policy;

- R&D and innovation strategy;

- increasing the public expenditure commitment to public and private R&D and innovation in an appropriately balanced way;

- managing the strategic R&D and Innovation Fund for public-private collaboration; and,

- encouraging increased funding for university research through block and other funds.

9.29   Such a unit could be the existing IRTU, or a new unit attached to one or more of the Departments, or a new central policy unit. One such structure that suggests itself under the proposed Government structures of the Multi-Party Agreement is that the Economic Policy Unit (EPU) in the Office of the First Minister and Deputy First Minister might include an Office of Science and Technology or Knowledge Economy Unit (KEU), with a Minister for Science, Technology and Innovation (MSTI). Or, the unit and Minister could be attached to a Department, such as the Department of Enterprise, Trade and Investment (DETI) or the Department of Higher and Further Education, Training and Employment (DHFETE), or both, or DFP. The EPU is a potential location of a Knowledge Economy Unit given the EPU's proposed role in supporting the First Minister and Deputy First Minister and the Executive Committee in the formulation, co-ordination and management of the policies and strategic goals of the Administration, in providing central economic policy initiatives, and in evaluating the effectiveness of programmes, policies and procedures of Departments, Boards and Agencies. But a strong case could also be made for locating the Ministerial Unit in DETI/DHFETE or DFP in order for it to retain the necessary full budgetary control.

Council for Science and Technology

9.30   A champion for R&D, S&T and innovation, as part of the overall economic development strategy in Northern Ireland, could protect funds for R&D and lobby for and take forward the R&D and knowledge-based economy agenda. The R&D lobby is currently not strong in Northern Ireland. In an 1981 report the Council recommended the establishment of a Council for the Application of Science and Technology in Northern Ireland (NIEC, 1981). In 1983 a report on R&D in Northern Ireland by Osola recommended a Technology Board for Northern Ireland which was duly set up in 1986. It was abolished when IRTU and its Board was established. Although the Board of IRTU is an effective channel of communication between industry, universities and Government as to R&D strategy, and does serve as an advisory board and champion of R&D, a more visible advisory board or council at arms-length from the Government, universities, industry and agriculture could perhaps serve a more effective role of advising on R&D and innovation policy.

9.31   A Council for Science, Technology and Innovation (CSTI) would be a potential institution to serve such a function. Such a Council's role would have to be carefully defined, but it would serve to advise Government on R&D, S&T and innovation policy as CST does in the UK, ICSTI does in the RoI, and the Royal Society of Edinburgh does in Scotland. It could advise on budgetary issues, on the role of S&T in economic development policy, on ICT in schools, on education, training and skills needs, on Foresight, and on the distribution of intramural R&D resources in Government.

Economic Development Agency

9.32   A focus on developing a knowledge-based economy in Northern Ireland must be reflected in the corporate plans of all of the Department's economic development agencies. *Strategy 2010* has proposed the creation of a single agency for economic development, combining the IDB, IRTU, LEDU and the company development programme of the T&EA. It will be important that such an agency puts R&D and innovation (the current focus of IRTU) and the needs of SMEs (the current focus of LEDU) at the forefront of its agenda, as argued recently by the Council (NIEC, 1999b). The creation of a single agency would be counterproductive if it was dominated by the current policies and priorities of IDB which, in many ways, is the lead agency. Any proposed single agency should be at arms-length from Government, along the lines of the Welsh Development Agency or Scottish Enterprise. Building the knowledge-based economy must permeate the policy of the Departments and any proposed agency, consistent with an enhanced role for R&D and innovation measures over subsidies to capital investment and job creation per se. The economic development strategy of the agency must be knowledge-driven.

9.33   One way that Northern Ireland can overcome its geographical and political isolation is to build an economy based on a holistic approach to knowledge production, capabilities and commercialisation rather than subsidy to the production of basic goods and services. A single and inclusive agency for economic development at arms-length from any single Government Department or Departments might be the best institutional form to guarantee such a holistic approach. The agency could have a strong policy co-ordination and implementation function around key priorities, which must of course include high profiles for R&D and innovation.   A single agency might be the best institutional innovation in order to create synergy and to avoid duplications of effort, such as the current various separate efforts to promote e-commerce in Northern Ireland Departments (DFP), agencies, (IRTU, LEDU and IDB), and universities (UU). The Board of Management of any proposed single agency should include prominent representation from the critical players in the knowledge-based economy and the regional R&D and innovation system, especially the universities and indigenous threshold SMEs but also international R&D and innovation partners.

Inter-Relationships

9.34   The relationship between a Knowledge Economy Unit, a Council for Science, Technology and Innovation, a Single Economic Development Agency, and the Departments, could be as follows. The Knowledge Economy Unit could act as a Secretariat to the Council and could produce an annual review of R&D and innovation in the economy, an annual R&D Budget, and a consolidated Single Programme for R&D. The Council could provide advice to Government on S&T and Innovation, which the Knowledge Economy Unit, the Economic Development Agency and the Departments, as well as any proposed Tertiary Sector Funding Council, would take into account in formulating R&D policy and a regional R&D and Innovation Strategy. The Economic Development Agency and the Departments could see to it that the strategy was implemented and continually monitored as to performance.

9.35   There could also be an Assembly Committee on Science, Technology and Innovation. The Chair of the Council for Science, Technology and Innovation could sit on this committee on a non-voting, advisory basis, along with the Director of the Knowledge Economy Unit in a similar capacity. Administrative arrangements for the new Northern Ireland Assembly provide for a North-South Ministerial Council with matters for co-operation involving R&D, including transport and strategic planning, agriculture, health, education, tourism and the environment. Implementation bodies will also be concerned with R&D matters, especially in food safety and in trade and business development (involving issues of R&D and innovation, enterprise, partnership and competitiveness). The exchange of information and co-ordination and co-operation in R&D will be on the agenda, as will collaboration on special EU programmes involving R&D. Specific initiatives might include a North-South Council for ICT or for Science, Technology and Innovation (or joint meetings of the ICSTI and a Northern Ireland Council for STI).

9.36   Figure 9A depicts how these various potential institutional arrangements could operate, and how the different institutions could relate to each other. The KEU could report to a Minister for Science,

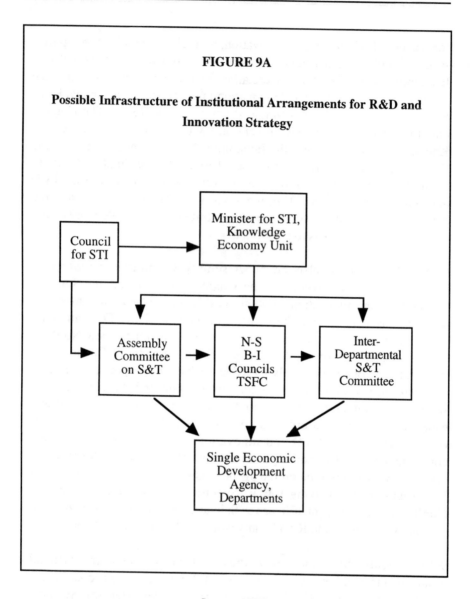

FIGURE 9A

Possible Infrastructure of Institutional Arrangements for R&D and Innovation Strategy

Source: NIEC

Technology and Innovation and would be a unit of the Economic Policy Unit of the Office of the First Minister and the Deputy First Minister or of the DETI/DHFETE. The unit could provide Secretariat services to an independent Council for Science, Technology and Innovation, to an Assembly Committee on Science and Technology, to an Inter-Departmental S&T Committee, to the North-South and British-Irish Councils in relation to S&T matters and to a Tertiary Sector Funding Council. On matters of Science, Technology and Innovation, the CSTI would then advise the MSTI, KEU, the Assembly Committee, the N-S and B-I Councils, the TSFC and the Inter-Departmental S&T Committee. The Single Economic Development Agency and the Departments would implement R&D, innovation and economic development policy. Such an arrangement would embed S&T matters of the knowledge-led economy at the heart of economic policy-making in Northern Ireland, exactly where they should be embedded.

Conclusion

9.37   An opportunity exists, with devolution, a new economic development strategy, and the pending establishment of a Science Park in Northern Ireland, to forge new partnerships in R&D, innovation and economic development between Government, industry, universities, and other public and private institutions, and to set new priorities in private and publicly funded R&D. The Science Park project along with a University Challenge Fund and a Northern Ireland R&D Challenge Fund should usher in a new era for R&D co-operation and collaboration in Northern Ireland. There is an undeniable sense that the R&D partners are willing to forge new alliances and strategies, but they need to be given the resources and institutions with which to do so. The Science Park will go some way to providing these means, but much more will need to be done, particularly in giving balanced attention to public as well as private R&D and innovation.

9.38   What is required is an institution of regional Government dedicated to the knowledge economy, a consensual R&D and innovation strategy for Northern Ireland, and the full embedding of this strategy into economic development strategy. The focus of public policy should be on facilitating capacities for collective action and co-ordination (Storper, 1995). A virtuous culture of co-ordination between R&D, innovation and economic development strategy must be built on a foundation of appropriate political and economic institutions and incentives for action (Putnam, 1993). The institutional innovations recommended in this section of the report would go some way to building this virtuous set of connections.

9.39   Innovation, partnership and enterprise must be the key principles upon which such a knowledge-led economic development strategy is founded. Government must work closely with both industry and higher education to determine appropriate institutions for setting priorities and targets, with corresponding actions, timetables and bench marks, and with appropriate lead agencies designated to carry these forward. Targets should be set that are achievable, along with well developed implementation plans to achieve those targets. Representative and inclusive agencies based on social and economic partnership must champion R&D, innovation, partnership and enterprise - all of which must become integral to the economic development strategy for Northern Ireland. Institutions and fora with the ability and means to take an overview of the public and private R&D and innovation system, within a knowledge-driven economic development strategy, must be considered. It is on this basis that the Council makes its recommendations.

9.40   What also must build on these initiatives as a next step is effort to instil a culture of risk-taking, innovation and entrepreneurship in public and private organisations in Northern Ireland, in order to lead to the business exploitation of R&D in Northern Ireland and to turn good research into good business. Incentives to encourage R&D, new venture capital initiatives, teaching entrepreneurship in business in schools, colleges and universities, knowledge networks, industry-education partnerships, and other ways to bring science and enterprise together, will all help to instil a culture of innovation and entrepreneurship.

9.41   The economic potential of Northern Ireland is strong. Effective knowledge management based on innovation, partnership and enterprise, both internally and externally to the region, must be marshalled to realise this potential. Northern Ireland must set up the institutions and instil the political and economic attitudes capable of sustaining it into the new millennium as a knowledge-driven economy.

REFERENCES

Beatty, E. K. (1997) "Some Examples of Best Practice in University-Industry Collaboration". Paper presented to CRI conference 'Partnership for Progress', Dublin, June.

Bennesworth, P. (1999) "The Future for Relations between Higher Education and RDAs". *Regions. The Newsletter of the Regional Studies Association*, No 220, April, p.15-22.

Best, M. (1995) *Competitive Dynamics and Industrial Modernisation Programmes: Lessons from Japan and America,* Annual Sir Charles Carter Lecture, Report 115, September. Belfast: Northern Ireland Economic Council.

Best, M. (1999, in process) *The Capabilities Perspective: Advancing Industrial Competitiveness in Northern Ireland.* Belfast: Northern Ireland Economic Council.

Blair, D. and Hitchins, D. (1998) *Campus Companies - UK and Ireland.* Aldershot, Hants: Ashgate Publishing Ltd.

Braczyk, H-J., Cooke, P. and Heidenreich, M., (eds) (1998) *Regional Innovation Systems: The Role of Governances in a Globalised World.* London: University College of London Press.

Cooke, P. (1996) "Enterprise Support Policies in Dynamic European Regions" in *Networking for Competitive Advantage*, Report No 100, November. Dublin: National Economic and Social Council.

Cooke, P. (1998) "The Role of Innovation in Regional Competitiveness". Prepared for the Conference on Cohesion, Competitiveness and Research, Technological Development and Innovation (RTDI); Their Impact on Regions, Maastricht, May 28-29. Cardiff: University of Wales, Centre for Advanced Studies.

Cooke, P. and Morgan, K. (1998) *The Associational Economy. Firms, Regions and Innovation.* Oxford: Oxford University Press.

Crone, M. and Roper, S. (1999) *Knowledge Transfers from Multinational Enterprise Plants in Northern Ireland.* Belfast: Northern Ireland Economic Research Centre.

CSO/SODoH (1998) *Research Strategy for the National Health Service in Scotland.* July. Edinburgh: Chief Scientist Office, Scottish Office Department of Health.

CST (1999) *Review of S&T Activity across Government Departments,* January. Notes by the Secretariat.

DANI (1996) *Research and Development Strategy 1996/97 to 1998/99.* Belfast: Department of Agriculture for Northern Ireland.

DANI (1998) *Science in DANI.* Belfast: The Department.

David, P. (1990) "The Dynamo and Computer: An Historical Perspective on the Modern Productivity Paradox", *American Economic Review, Papers and Proceedings,* Vol 80, No 2, May, pp.355-361.

Davies, M. L. (1997) *Review of DANI R&D,* September. Belfast: IRTU.

DED (1992) *Innovation 2000: A Research and Development Strategy for Northern Ireland.* Belfast: The Department.

DED (1995) *Growing Competitively.* Belfast: The Department.

DED (1997) *Northern Ireland Civil and Defence Expenditure on Research and Development During 1996.* Belfast: The Department.

DED (1999) *Facts and Figures from the Inter-Departmental Business Registrar (IDBR)*, Edition One - May 1999. Belfast: DED Statistics Research Branch.

DEE (1996) *Science, Technology and Innovation: The White Paper.* Dublin: Department of Enterprise and Employment, Office of Science and Technology, the Stationery Office.

DENI (1999) *Lifelong Learning: The Funding, Planning and Management of the Further and Higher Education Sectors: Consultation Paper.* Bangor: Training and Employment Agency and Department of Education for Northern Ireland.

DFP (1998) *Public Expenditure in Northern Ireland 1999-00 to 2001-02: A Consultation Paper.* Belfast: Department of Finance and Personnel.

DFP/HM Treasury (1998) *Northern Ireland Expenditure Plans and Priorities, The Government's Expenditure Plans 1998-1999*, Cm 3916. London: Stationery Office.

DFP/HM Treasury (1999) *Northern Ireland Expenditure Plans and Priorities. The Government's Expenditure Plans 1999-2000 to 2001-2002*, Cm 4217. London: Stationery Office.

DoE (NI) (1998) *Shaping Our Future. Draft Regional Strategic Framework for Northern Ireland.* Belfast: Department of the Environment for Northern Ireland.

DTI (1993) *Realising our Potential: A Strategy for Science, Engineering and Technology*, Cm 2250. London: Chancellor of the Duchy of Lancaster, HMSO.

DTI (1998) *Our Competitive Future: Building the Knowledge Driven Economy.* White Paper and Analytical Report, Cm 4176. London: Department of Trade and Industry.

DTI (1999) *Regional Competitiveness Indicators,* February. London: Department of Trade and Industry.

DTI/ONS (1998) *Science, Engineering and Technology Statistics*, Cm 4006, July. London: The Stationery Office.

Dunford, M. and Hudson, R. (1996) *Successful European Regions: Northern Ireland Learning form Others.* Research Monograph 3, November. Belfast: Northern Ireland Economic Council.

Dunning, J., Bannerman, E. and Lundan, S. (1998) *Competitiveness and Industrial Policy in Northern Ireland.* Research Monograph 5, March. Belfast: Northern Ireland Economic Council.

EC (1995) "Green Paper on Innovation", *Bulletin of the European Union,* Supplement 5/95. Luxembourg: European Commission.

EC (1997) "The First Action Plan for Innovation in Europe". *Bulletin of the European Union.* Supplement 3/97. Luxembourg: European Commission.

EC (1998) "Reinforcing Cohesion and Competitiveness through RTD and Innovation Policies", Cm (98) 275, 27 May. Brussels: European Commission.

Economic Council of Canada (1992) *Pulling Together: Productivity, Innovation and Trade.* Ottawa: Economic Council of Canada.

Economic Development Strategy Review Steering Group (1999) *Strategy 2010.* Belfast: Department of Economic Development.

Feldman, M. (1994) *The Geography of Innovation.* Dordrecht, The Netherlands: Kluwer Academic Publishers.

Fitz Gerald, J., Kearney, I., Morgenroth, E. and Smyth, D. (1999) *National Investment Priorities for the Period 2000-2006*. Policy Research Series 33. Dublin: Economic and Social Research Institute.

Forfás (1998) *State Investment in Science and Technology, 1998*, September. Dublin: Forfás.

Freeman, C. (1994) "Innovation and Growth", in Dobson, M. and Rothwell, R. (eds) *The Handbook of Industrial Innovation*. Cheltenham: Edward Elgar

Griliches, Z. (1995) "R&D and Productivity: Econometric Results and Measurement Issues". In Stoneman, P. (ed) *Handbook of the Economics of Innovation and Technological Change*. Oxford: Blackwell Press.

Hamilton, S. F. and Sunding, D. L. (1998) "Returns to Public Investments in Agriculture with Imperfect Downstream Competition". *American Journal of Agricultural Economics*, November, pp.830-838.

HEFCE (1998) *Industry-Academic Links in the UK*. 98/70, December. Bristol: Higher Education Funding Council for England.

HEFCE (1999) *Higher Education Reach-out to Business and Community Fund. Funding Proposals*. 99/16. Bristol: Higher Education Funding Council for England.

HM Treasury (1998) *Modern Public Services for Britain: Investing in Reform. Comprehensive Spending Review: New Public Spending Plans 1999-2002*, July, Cm 4001. London: the Stationery Office.

HM Treasury/DTI (1998) *Innovating for the Future: Investing in R&D*. London: HM Treasury, Department of Trade and Industry.

HPSS (1999) *Research for Health and Wellbeing: A Strategy for R&D to Lead Northern Ireland into the 21st Century*. Belfast: R&D Office.

Hudson, R. (1999) "The Learning Economy, the Learning Firm and the Learning Region: A Sympathetic Critique of the Limits of Learning", *European Urban and Regional Studies*, Vol 6 (1), pp.59-72.

Hughes, A. E. (1998) *Review of the External Research Income of the Northern Ireland Universities; Final Report.* A Report to the Northern Ireland Higher Education Council, October.

ICSTI (1998a) *Mechanism for Prioritisation of State Expenditures on Science and Technology*, June. Dublin: Forfás.

ICSTI (1998b) *State Expenditure Priorities for 1999*, November. Dublin: Forfás.

ICSTI (1999a) *Investing in Research, Technology and Innovation (RTI) in the Period 2000 to 2006*, January. Dublin. Forfás

ICSTI (1999b) *Technology Foresight Ireland*, April. Dublin: Forfás.

IDB (1998) *Corporate Plan 1998-2001.* Belfast: Industrial Development Board.

IRTU (1998) *Corporate Plan 1998-2001.* Belfast: Industrial Research and Technology Unit.

Katz, M. and Shapiro, C. (1994) "Systems Competition and Network Effects". *Journal of Economic Perspectives*, Vol 8, No 2, Spring, pp.93-115.

Keeble, D. and Wilkinson, F. (eds.) (1999) "Special Issue: Regional Networking, Collective Learning and Innovation in High Technology SMEs in Europe". *Regional Studies*, Vol 33, No 4, June.

Khatri, Y. and Thirtle, C. (1996) "Supply and Demand Functions for UK Agriculture: Biases of Technical Change and the Returns to Public R&D". *Journal of Agricultural Economics*, September, pp.338-354.

Kinsella, R. P. and McBierty, V. J. (1995) *Economic Rationale for an Enhanced National Science and Technology Capability.* Dublin: Forfás.

Lipsey, R. G. (1993) *Globalisation, Technological Change and Economic Growth,* Annual Sir Charles Carter Lecture. Report 103, July. Belfast: Northern Ireland Economic Council.

Lopez-Bassols, V. (1998) "How R&D is Changing", *OECD Observer,* 213 August/September, pp.16-18.

Lundvall, B-A. (ed) (1992) *National Systems of Innovation: Towards a Theory of Innovation and Interactive Learning.* London: Pinter.

Martin, B. and Salter, A. et al (1996) *The Relationship between Public Funded Basic Research and Economic Performance: An SPRU Review,* July. Science Policy Research Unit, University of Sussex.

Maskell, P. and Malmberg, A. (1999) "The Competitiveness of Firms and Regions: 'Ubiquitification' and the Importance of Localised Learning", *European Urban and Regional Studies,* Vol 6 (1), pp.9-25.

Maskell, P. et al (1998) *Competitiveness, Localised Learning and Regional Development: Specialisation and Prosperity in Small Open Economies.* London: Routledge.

McKenna, G. and Hogg, B. (1998) "Lack of Research Funding for Northern Ireland's Universities is a Major Threat to Economic Recovery". Mimeo. Jordanstown/Belfast: UU/QUB.

Morgan, K. (1997) "The Learning Region: Institutions, Innovation and Regional Renewal", *Regional Studies,* 31 (5), pp.491-504.

NCIHE (1997) *Higher Education in the Learning Society,* July. London: National Committee of Inquiry into Higher Education, Chairman, Sir Ron Dearing CB.

NESC (1998) *Sustaining Competitive Advantage: Proceedings of a NESC Seminar.* NESC Research Series, March. Dublin: National Economic and Social Council.

NIEC (1981) *Research and Development and Innovation in Northern Ireland.* Report 125. Belfast: Northern Ireland Economic Council.

NIEC (1993) *R&D Activity in Northern Ireland.* Report 101, May. Belfast: Northern Ireland Economic Council.

NIEC (1997) *The 1997 UK Budget: Implications for Northern Ireland.* Report 125. Belfast: Northern Ireland Economic Council.

NIEC (1998) *A Framework for Economic Development: The Implications for Northern Ireland of the 1998 UK and EU Budgets and the Chancellor's Economic Strategy for Northern Ireland.* Report 127. Belfast: Northern Ireland Economic Council.

NIEC (1999a) *Let's Get Together. Linkages and Inward Investment in Northern Ireland.* Report 130. Belfast: Northern Ireland Economic Council.

NIEC (1999b) *The Implementation of Northern Ireland's Development Strategy in the 1990s. Lessons for the Future.* Report 131. Belfast: Northern Ireland Economic Council.

NIGC (1995) *Interim Summary of Progress.* Belfast: Northern Ireland Growth Challenge.

NIHEC (1999) *Draft Consultation Paper on the Research Funding Allocation Methodology to be Applied to the Northern Ireland Universities.* Bangor: NIHEC.

OECD (1998a) *Technology, Productivity and Job Creation: Best Policy Practices.* Paris: Organisation for Economic Co-operation and Development.

OECD (1998b) *University Research in Transition.* Paris: Organisation for Economic Co-operation and Development.

OECD (1998c) *Main Science and Technology Indicators.* Paris: Organisation for Economic Co-operation and Development.

OECD (1999) *OECD in Figures.* Paris: Organisation for Economic Co-operation and Development.

ONS (1998a) "Research and Experimental Development (R&D) Statistics 1996" *Economic Trends* No 537, August. London: Office for National Statistics, HMSO.

ONS (1998b) "UK Results from the Community Innovation Survey". *Economic Trends*, No 539, October. London: Office for National Statistics, HMSO.

ONS (1998c) *Regional Trends.* London: Office for National Statistics, HMSO.

ONS (1999) *Social Trends.* London: Office for National Statistics, HMSO.

Osola (1983) *A Critical Review of Industrial Research and Development Support Facilities in Northern Ireland.* Worcester: J Osola and Associates.

OST (1997) *The Use of Scientific Advice in Policy Making*, March. London: Department of Trade and Industry.

OST (1998) *The Use of Scientific Advice in Policy Making: Implementation of the Guidelines*, July. London: Department of Trade and Industry.

OST (1999) *The Forward Look 1999: Government-Funded Science, Engineering and Technology*, Cm 4363. London: The Stationery Office.

OST/DTI (1996) *Review of the Inter-Relationships between Science, Engineering and Technology Expenditures of Government Departments*, December. London: Department of Trade and Industry.

Pianta, M. (1995) "Technology and Growth in OECD Countries 1970-1990" *Cambridge Journal of Economics,* Vol 19, No 1, pp.175-87.

Pilat, D. (1998) "The Economic Impact of Technology", *OECD Observer,* 213 August/September, pp.5-8.

Porter, M. (1990) *The Competitive Advantage of Nations.* New York: The Free Press.

Porter, M. (1998) "The Microeconomic Foundations of Economic Development" in *The Global Competitiveness Report 1998.* Geneva: World Economic Forum.

Putnam, R. (1993) *Making Democracy Work.* New Jersey: Princeton University Press.

QUB (1997) *Report of the Strategic Review Group*, December. Belfast: The Queen's University of Belfast.

RIS/Yorkshire and the Humber (1999) *Regional Innovation Strategy for Yorkshire and the Humber: The Report.* Batley, West Yorkshire: RIS Secretariat.

Robson, B. et al (1997) "Higher Education and Regions", Background Report 9 of *Higher Education in the Learning Society*, July. London: National Committee of Inquiry into Higher Education, Chairman, Sir Ron Dearing CB.

Romer, Paul (1986) "Increasing Returns and Long-Run Growth". *Journal of Political Economy*, Vol 94, pp.1002-37.

Romer, Paul (1994) "The Origins of Endogenous Growth". *Journal of Economic Perspectives*, Vol 8, No 1, Winter, pp.3-22.

Roper, S. and Hewitt-Dundas, N. (1998) *Innovation, Networks and the Diffusion of Manufacturing Best Practice: A Comparison of Northern Ireland and the Republic of Ireland*, Research Report 40. Belfast: Northern Ireland Economic Research Centre.

Scottish Enterprise (1996) *Technology Ventures: Commercialising Scotland's Science and Technology*. Edinburgh: Scottish Enterprise and The Royal Society of Edinburgh.

Scottish Office (1999) *Scotland: Towards the Knowledge Economy*. Report of the Knowledge Economy Taskforce, April. Glasgow: Scottish Office.

SIF (1999) *ITs the Future: A Strategy for the Software Industry in Northern Ireland*. Belfast: Software Industry Federation.

SQW (1996) *Review of the Funding of University Research in Northern Ireland, Phase 1 - Final Report.* London: Segal Quince Wicksteed Ltd.

SQW (1997) *Review of the Funding of University Research in Northern Ireland, Phase II - Final Report.* London: Segal Quince Wicksteed Ltd.

Storper, M. (1995) "The Resurgence of Regional Economies, Ten Years Later: The Region as a Nexus of Untraded Interdependencies", *European Urban and Regional Studies*, Vol 2 (3), pp.191-221.

Storper, M. (1997) *The Regional World*. New York: Guildford Press.

Thanki, R. (1999) "How Do We Know the Value of Higher Education to Regional Development?" *Regional Studies*, 33 (2) pp.84-89.

The Economist (1999) *Survey: Innovation in Industry*, February 20.

UU (1998) *Outline Proposal Submitted to DED on Establishing Science Parks in Northern Ireland*. Coleraine: University of Ulster.

Vickery, G. (1999) "Business and Industry Policies for Knowledge-Based Economies", *OECD Observer* 215, January, pp.9-11.

WDA (1998) *Wales Regional Technology Plan: An Innovation and Technology Strategy for Wales, Review and Update*. Cardiff: Welsh Development Agency.

LIST OF PERSONS CONSULTED

NAME	ORGANISATION
Ingrid Allen	RDO, HPSS, Belfast
Eric Beatty	QUB, Belfast
Susanne Bjerregard	Advanced Technology Group, Denmark
Robin Boyd	DANI, Belfast
Alex Boyle	DoE (NI), Belfast
Alistair Bradley	DENI, Bangor
Marcus Breathnach	Forfás, Dublin
Joe Brown	Scottish Office, Edinburgh
Linda Brown	DoE (NI), Belfast
Peter Bunn	DTI, London
John Coote	NIHEC, Bangor
Joanne Donaldson	OST, London
David Elton	CST, London
Michael Fitzgibbon	Forfás, Dublin
Tom Fleming	Government Office of the North East, Newcastle
Fiona Hepper	DED, Statistics Branch
Brian Hogg	QUB, Belfast
Richard Holmes	NIHEC, Bangor
Peter Holmes	DENI, Bangor
Edgar Jardine	NISRA, Belfast
Peter Jones	Office for National Statistics, Newport
Alistair Keddie	DTI, London
Ian Lomax	OST, London

NAME	ORGANISATION
Ron Loveland	Welsh Office, Cardiff
Greg McConnell	IRTU, Lisburn
Shawn McCormick	IRTU, Lisburn
Gerry McKenna	UU, Coleraine
Cecil McMurray	DANI, Belfast
Andrew Meads	DED, Belfast
Chris Morris	DHSS, Belfast
Mike Nalley	DTI, London
Michael Neely	RDO, HPSS, Belfast
Tony Newson	Welsh Development Agency, Cardiff
Dermot O'Doherty	Forfás, Dublin
Bernie O'Hare	IRTU, Lisburn
Tomas Olofsson	Teknopol, Lund, Sweden
Michael Pender	DETI, Dublin
Bert Rima	RDO, HPSS, Belfast
Stephen Roper	NIERC, Belfast
Andrew Rushworth	SOAEF, Edinburgh
Philip Rycroft	Scottish Office, Edinburgh
Mark Sinclair	OST, London
Alison Spaull	CSO, SODoH, Edinburgh
Noreen Taggart	UU, Coleraine
Arie Van Heeringen	AWT, the Netherlands
Roland Wickstrom	Teknopol, Lund, Sweden

PROJECT STAFF

Research: .... Peter Wylie

Text Processor and Editor: .... Roisin Rogers

Proof-reader: .... Roy Boreland

NIEC PUBLICATIONS IN THE LAST 5 YEARS

Reports

115   Annual Sir Charles Carter Lecture "Competitive Dynamics and Industrial Modernisation Programmes: Lessons from Japan and America" by Michael H Best, Centre for Industrial Competitiveness, University of Massachusetts, Lowell (September 1995)

116   Annual Report 1994-95 (October 1995)

117   Taxes, Benefits, Unemployment and Poverty Traps in Northern Ireland (November 1995)

118   The 1995 UK Budget: Background and Implications for Northern Ireland (February 1996)

119   Annual Report 1995-96 (October 1996)

120   Annual Sir Charles Carter Lecture "Reforming Education in the United Kingdom: The Vital Priorities" by Sir Claus Moser KCB CBE FBA, The British Museum Development Trust (January 1997)

121   Rising to the Challenge: The Future of Tourism in Northern Ireland (February 1997)

122   The 1996 UK Budget: Implications for Northern Ireland (March 1997)

123   Industrial Policy Assessment and Performance Measurement - The Case of the IDB (April 1997)

124   Annual Report 1996-97 (October 1997)

125   The 1997 UK Budget: Implications for Northern Ireland (November 1997)

126   Annual Sir Charles Carter Lecture "Setting Priorities for Health Care: Why Government Should Take the Lead" by Chris Ham, Professor of Health Policy and Management and Director, Health Services Management Centre, University of Birmingham (January 1998)

127   A Framework for Economic Development: The Implications for Northern Ireland of the 1998 UK and EU Budgets and the Chancellor's Economic Strategy for Northern Ireland (June 1998)

128   Annual Report 1997-98 (October 1998)

129   Annual Sir Charles Carter Lecture "Social Exclusion, Income Dynamics and Public Policy" by Professor John Hills, Director, Centre for Analysis of Social Exclusion, London School of Economics and Political Science (April 1999)

130   Let's Get Together. Linkages and Inward Investment in Northern Ireland (June 1999)

131   The Implementation of Northern Ireland's Economic Development Strategy in the 1990s: Lessons for the Future (August 1999)

132   Annual Report 1998-99 (October 1999)

Occasional Paper Series

1   Reforming the Educational System in Northern Ireland. A Comment on 'Learning for Life' and Recent Developments in the Education System (January 1995)

2   Demographic Trends in Northern Ireland: Key Findings and Policy Implications (March 1995)

3   "Through Peace to Prosperity". Proceedings of the Peace Seminar hosted by the Economic Council (April 1995)

4   The Economic Implications of Peace and Political Stability for Northern Ireland (June 1995)

*   A *Supplementary Paper* to NIEC *Occasional Paper 4:-*
     The Implications of Peace and Political Stability in Northern Ireland for Selected Sectors: Inward Investment, Tourism and Security (June 1995)

5   Health and Personal Social Services to the Millennium. A Response to *Regional Strategy for Health and Social Wellbeing, 1997-2002* (December 1995)

6   Building A Better Future: A Response to *Building on Success. Proposals for Future Housing Policy* (May 1996)

7   "Decentralised Government and Economic Performance in Northern Ireland". Proceedings of the Seminar sponsored by the Northern Ireland Economic Council in association with the University of Ulster on 19 June 1996 at the University of Ulster at Jordanstown (December 1996)

8   Towards Resolving Long-Term Unemployment in Northern Ireland. A Response to the *Long-Term Unemployment Consultation Document* (June 1997)

9   The Impact of a National Minimum Wage on the Northern Ireland Economy. A Response to the Low Pay Commission (February 1998)

10   "Hard Choices. Policy Autonomy and Priority-setting in Public Expenditure". Proceedings of the Seminar sponsored by the Northern Ireland Economic Council jointly with Democratic Dialogue and the Eastern Health and Social Services Board on 22 June 1998 at the Eastern Health and Social Services Board (November 1998)

11   Growth with Development. A Response to New TSN (December 1998)

12   A Step-Change in Economic Performance? A Response to *Strategy 2010* (September 1999)

Research Monograph Series

1   Demographic Review Northern Ireland 1995 by Paul Compton (March 1995)

2   The Arts and the Northern Ireland Economy by John Myerscough with A Statement by the Economic Council (January 1996)

3   Successful European Regions: Northern Ireland Learning From Others by Michael Dunford and Ray Hudson with A Statement by the Economic Council (November 1996)

4   Educational Achievement in Northern Ireland: Patterns and Prospects by Tony Gallagher, Ian Shuttleworth and Colette Gray with a Statement by the Economic Council (December 1997)

5   Competitiveness and Industrial Policy in Northern Ireland by John H Dunning, Edward Bannerman and Sarianna M Lundan with A Statement by the Economic Council (March 1998)

6   Regional Economic and Policy Impacts of EMU: The Case of Northern Ireland, edited by John Bradley with A Statement by the Economic Council (April 1998)

7   Improving Schools in Northern Ireland by Tony Gallagher, Ian Shuttleworth and Colette Gray with A Statement by the Economic Council (August 1998)

Advice and Comment Series

98/1   A Response by the Northern Ireland Economic Council to:
        Northern Ireland Science Park (Department of Economic Development) September 1998 *(3 pages)*

98/2   A Response by the Northern Ireland Economic Council to:
        Fit for the Future (Department of Health and Social Services) September 1998 *(13 pages)*

98/3   A Response by the Northern Ireland Economic Council to:
        Structural Funds Plan 2000-2006 (Department of Finance and Personnel) October 1998 *(2 pages)*

98/4   A Response by the Northern Ireland Economic Council to:
        Housing Selection Scheme Review: Proposals for Consultation (Northern Ireland Housing Executive) October 1998 *(12 pages)*

99/1   A Response by the Northern Ireland Economic Council to:
        Water and Sewerage Services in Northern Ireland: A Consultation Paper (Department of the Environment for Northern Ireland) February 1999 *(11 pages)*

99/2   A Response by the Northern Ireland Economic Council to:
        Shaping Our Future. Towards a Strategy for the Development of the Region (Department of the Environment for Northern Ireland) April 1999 *(16 pages)*